Turning Holiday Ornaments

Selected Readings from *American Woodturner*,
journal of the American Association of Woodturners

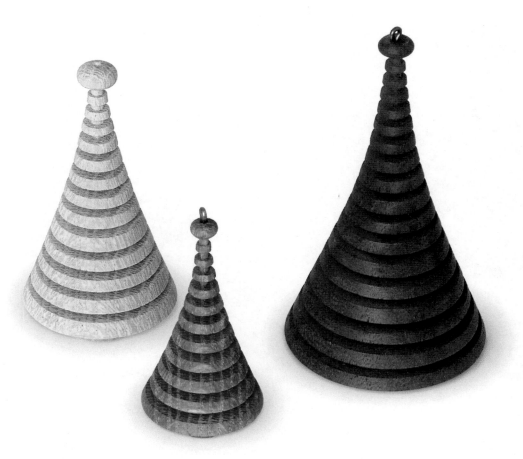

American Association of Woodturners
222 Landmark Center
75 5th St. W
St. Paul, MN 55102-7704
877-595-9094
www.woodturner.org

Contents

Published by American Association of Woodturners,
222 Landmark Center, 75 5th St. W., St. Paul, MN 55102-7704.
877-595-9094, www.woodturner.org.

American Woodturner (ISSN 0895-9005) is published bimonthly by American Association of Woodturners.

Turning Holiday Ornaments
ISBN 978-1-939662-09-5

Printed on Demand in United States of America
American Association of Woodturners, www.woodturner.org

Introduction

Holiday woodturning projects are so popular because they are interesting, skill-building and perhaps challenging to make. They are always fun to give, and they are a delight to receive. Better yet, they are unique expressions—no-one will find another at the mall.

Some turners try to design and make a different ornament for each gift recipient. Others make an edition—snowmen for everyone this year, Santas next. Either way, woodturning can help you with your gift-giving list.

Simple projects invite repetition, which is a gift given back to the woodturner, because practice is the best way to build turning skills. More complex projects, like inside-out profile turned trees and Santa nutcrackers, build skills in another way, by requiring accurate work on multiple parts that need to fit together.

Professional turners find that not only do they need to continue making batches of popular ornaments to sell in each holiday season, they also need to come up with something new. The designs in this book may be reproduced by individual turners without restriction, though credit to the originator is always appreciated. These designs also can be jumping off points for variations and new ideas of your own.

Whatever your family tradition, holiday ornaments make great gifts. Everyone loves hand-worked wood, so you can be sure that families and friends will enjoy receiving holiday ornaments from your lathe.

Selected Readings
from *AW Journal*

From its founding in 1986, the American Association of Woodturners has published a regular journal of advice, information and good fellowship for everyone interested in the field. Led by a series of dedicated editors and board members, the *AW Journal* has evolved to become *American Woodturner* magazine, now published in full color six times each year.

The *AW Journal* is a genuine treasure trove of practical, shop-tested information written by woodturners for their fellow woodturners. *Turning Holiday Ornaments* is the fifth volume in an ongoing series being extracted from this archive. *Turning Holiday Ornaments* is available as a 64-page printed book, or as a digital e-book readable on all your electronic devices.

Holiday Ornaments

AAW Members

Third Place
Bill Lewis, *Touch of Gold Christmas*, 2011, Maple, TomBow color, Prismacolor paint, 2-3/4" × 2" (7 cm × 5 cm)

Holiday Ornaments Challenge

These lovely ornaments were made in 2011 by members of the American Association of Woodturners in response to an on-line challenge to create new holiday ornaments. Jurors for this challenge were Kurt Bird, forum moderator, and woodturner John Lucas.

Member forums on the American Association of Woodturners website often invite members to participate in woodturning challenges like this. It's one of the many benefits of membership in the non-profit organization. To find out more, go to woodturner.org.

First Place
Ed McDonnell, Untitled, 2011, Loquat, atomized copper, 8" × 2" (20 cm × 5 cm)

Second Place
Curtis Fuller, Untitled, 2011, Bethlehem olive, walnut, 6-1/4" × 1-3/4" (15 cm × 4 cm)

Michael Gibson, Untitled, 2011, Pear, African blackwood, 6" (15 cm) high

Roger Meeker, *Jetsons Holiday Ornament*, 2011, Pine, brass rod, paint, 7-3/4" × 3" × 4-3/4" (20 cm × 8 cm × 12 cm)

Bob Davis,
Nutcracker, 2011,
Maple, acrylic,
3-3/4" × 1-1/2"
(10 cm × 4 cm)

Bernie Hrytzak,
That's a Wrap, 2011,
Spruce, acrylic paint,
3" × 1-1/4" (7 cm × 3.5 cm)

Scott Hackler,
Untitled, 2011,
Quilted maple,
African blackwood,
5" × 1-3/4" (13 cm × 4 cm)

Hal Taylor,
Angel, 2011,
Bradford pear, paint,
6-1/2" × 5-1/4"
(17 cm × 13 cm)

John Beaver,
Open Wave, 2011,
Walnut, maple, milk paint,
8" × 4" (20 cm × 10 cm)

Joseph Geiner,
Untitled, 2011,
Mahogany,
7-1/2" × 2-1/2"
(19 cm × 6 cm)

Michael Gibson,
Untitled, 2011,
Pear, dye,
6-1/2" (17 cm) high

Curtis Fuller,
Angel, 2011,
Birch plywood, poplar, aspen,
5" × 4" (13 cm × 10 cm)

Martin van der Sanden,
Untitled, 2011,
Cedar,
9-3/4" × 3" (25 cm × 8 cm)

North Coast Tree

Bob Rosand

Several years ago when I demonstrated for the North Coast Woodturners chapter in Ohio, I stayed at the home of George and Pat Raeder. While there, George presented me with his version of a turned Christmas tree. I saw a lot of beauty in this simple, yet intriguing, design.

George's tree hung in my shop until the date for our holiday open house approached. As usual, I was looking for that elusive easy-to-turn, inexpensive, fast-selling item as an ornament or bobble for a wrapped gift. George's Christmas tree filled the bill perfectly!

You can make these trees either free-standing or as ornaments with screw eyes.

Get started

To complete this project, you will need a 1/2" or 3/4" spindle roughing gouge, a 3/8" spindle gouge, a standard parting tool, a 1/2" skew (optional), and a thin parting tool. The standard parting tool tends to tear the wood fibers a bit. For the clean and fine cuts required, the thin-walled 1/16" parting tool is ideal because the flutes slice through the wood. Many woodturning catalogs show this tool, which is often attributed to Nick Cook.

You can turn this tree to any height. I've made them anywhere from 2" tall to about 8–9" tall. A good size blank to start with is about 2 × 2 × 5".

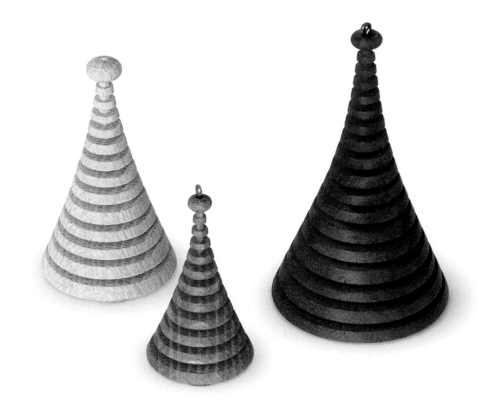

Turn your tree

With your center finder, locate the center of each end of your blank, and place it between the centers of your lathe. Use the spindle roughing gouge to true up the blank. Then switch to a 1/2" skew or parting tool to turn a tenon to hold the blank in a 4-jaw chuck.

If you don't have a chuck, fasten a waste block to a small faceplate, and glue the tree stock to that. The end result will be the same; it's just a bit more time consuming.

With the tree blank held firmly in a 4-jaw scroll chuck, bring up the tail center for safety. Then shape the

tree with a spindle roughing gouge. The top of the tree should be toward the tailstock and the bottom of the tree toward the headstock. The spindle roughing gouge is ideal for roughing stock, but used properly, it is also a good tool for making long, smooth curves, or in this case, Christmas trees.

When you have the shape of the tree about where you want it, use your spindle gouge to turn a small finial (about 1/2" or 3/8") on what will be the top of the tree *(Photo 1)*. If you are going to make a hanging ornament out of this tree, now is a good time to pull back the

AW 22:4, p32

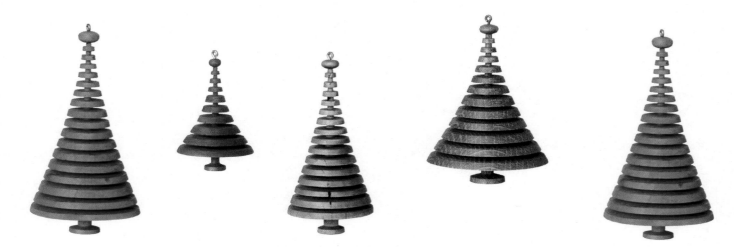

tailstock and drill a 1/16" or smaller hole in the top of the tree/finial so that you can later insert a screw eye. Once completed, bring up the tailstock again.

Resharpen your spindle roughing gouge and then refine the shape of the tree. For this task, I have good results using the tool on its side. If you look at the gouge from its front, the spindle roughing gouge has two flat edges. (I find these to be the most useful for long, smooth curves.) Sand lightly with 120-grit or 150-grit sandpaper.

Get in the groove

Now the fun part—cutting the grooves (branch rings) into the tree. Make your first parting cut at the base of the finial (top of the tree) and leave a tree trunk of about 1/8" diameter.

Make further cuts until you approach the base of the ornament (Photo 2). The trick is consistency. Each branch ring should be the same thickness as the previous one, and the trunk of the tree should be consistent. Light sanding is appropriate. But be careful, as the tree is delicate.

With a standard parting tool, form the base of the tree stand and then part from the lathe (Photo 3). Insert a #214-1/2 brass screw eye or snipped-off fish hook into the finial and your tree is nearly done.

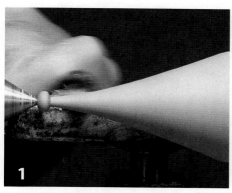

Use a spindle roughing gouge on its side to refine the shape of the finial.

Color options

The wood's natural look is fine as is, but I look for variations on a theme. One option is to stir up colored dyes and soak the trees in them. I've had good results with Arti Toymaker's and TransFast dyes, available in powder form from most woodworking catalogs. When dry, spray the trees with lacquer and lightly buff.

George pointed out to me that you could sand some of the dye from the outside of the tree, leaving the inner surface darker.

Have fun making your trees, and let me know if you come up with any great variations.

Bob Rosand is a professional turner and educator living in Bloomsburg, PA. He has been a frequent contributor to the AW Journal.

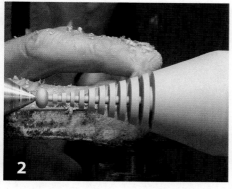

Cut the branch rings with a thin parting tool and leave a 1/8"-diameter tree trunk.

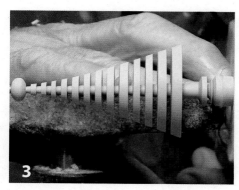

Create a stand for the tree and part the ornament from the chuck.

Eccentric Trees

David Reed Smith

Usually, I remember where I found the idea for a project. But this time, I don't. I started working on eccentric trees right after turning a batch of "North Coast" trees popularized by Bob Rosand.

These are quick and inexpensive to turn from construction-grade lumber (unless you're trying to take the ornament upscale). They're easy to turn if you're comfortable with a skew and off-center mounting, and are good practice if you're not. If you're truly terrified of the skew you can use a different tool, although it will be slower.

Here's a quick overview of the turning steps: Mount the ornament between centers and turn a tree shape. Then mount the tree with the base slightly offset (eccentric) at three equally spaced intervals to create "branches." After accenting the branches with acrylic paint, re-chuck the ornament, clean up the tree profile, and turn the angel top and base.

You could turn the entire tree between centers, but I find it easier to do the last turning with the ornament mounted in a chuck. This allows me to finish, drill, and sand the angel's head on the lathe.

A variety of basic tree shapes provides plenty of creative variations to these ornaments turned on three eccentric positions.

Get started

For turning tools, you'll need a 1" skew, a 3/4" spindle roughing gouge, and a parting tool.

To make the best use of your time (unless you're making a big batch of ornaments) it helps to easily switch to the off-center positions without removing the chuck. I use a home-made drive center that mounts in my Beall collet chuck.

For the tailstock, it's nice to have a center that will limit penetration and avoid splitting the stock. I used a washer, but there are other ways. (For a discussion of methods for chucking and tailstocks see my website at davidreedsmith.com.)

AW 23:4, p26

For turning stock, construction-grade pine or Douglas fir is ideal because it's light and inexpensive. For the first project, create a 1-1/2 × 1-1/2 × 6" block.

Turn the tree

Allow a generous extra amount for mounting a tenon in the chuck and a nub at the tailstock end that won't tend to split.

Take the time to make a clean crosscut on at least one end of the turning square, as it's easier to mount to a center you can see. Mark the center of the square at both ends. Dimple the mark with a centerpunch to help you find the mark on the lathe. On the tailstock end, draw three equally spaced lines radiating from the center mark (Photo 1). Then make a mark on each line equally spaced from the center. (After you turn your first tree, experiment with different distances to find what looks best to you; 3/16" is a good distance to start with.) Mark each distance with a centerpunch.

Mount the turning square between centers and use a spindle roughing gouge to reduce the square to a cylinder. Use a parting tool and calipers to size a tenon at the headstock end that will fit your chuck. Make another cut with the parting tool to mark the base of the tree. With a spindle roughing gouge or skew, reduce the full tenon to the marked diameter.

With a spindle roughing gouge, reduce the diameter at the tailstock end to a little more than the diameter of the finished finial (about ½"). Define the bottom of the finial with a parting tool or skew cut. Allow a generous extra amount for a nub that won't split (Photo 2).

Now shape the tree with a 3/4" spindle roughing gouge. Pick any simple shape that you like. I think the trees look equally attractive with a straight, convex, or concave profile.

It's a good practice to skim the surface with a skew.

With a pencil, mark off intervals for the branches (Photo 3). You can use regular or graduated intervals; just don't make them random or much less than 1/4" apart. (Experience has taught me that the trees look better when the branches are marked.)

Go eccentric

At the headstock end, remount the blank at one of the offset locations. Leave the tailstock at the same center, which will make the branches taper near the top. This also reduces the likelihood that you'll accidentally part off the top of the tree. Normally a 2-prong center is best for offset turning, but since the shift is small and pine is soft, a cup drive works fine. Rotate the lathe by hand to make sure the tree clears the tool rest.

Use your skew to make a V-cut at the branch location marked closest to the bottom (Photo 4). Keep the side of the cut at the tailstock side more or less vertical. Cut until it looks like you're cutting as deep as the ghost image. You actually cut about two-thirds of the way around the tree, which has a pleasing appearance. If you do end up cutting deeper than you planned, make adjustments during the last turning.

If you're uneasy about making V-cuts with a skew, you can create the V-cuts with a spindle gouge. Roll the gouge so that the flute faces straight to your right. Hold the gouge so that the axis of the shaft points straight to the axis of the ornament, point the bevel of the gouge where you want to go, and push in a little bit. Roll the gouge over so it points straight to your left and aim the bevel to about where the last cut ended up and repeat until the V-cut is as deep as you like. Practice this first on non-offset work.

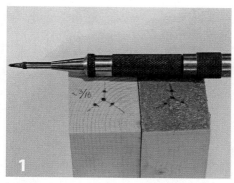

With a centerpunch, mark offset centers on the headstock end of the turning square.

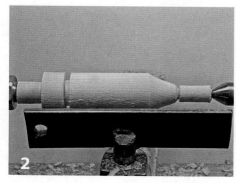

Rough-turn the shape and add a 1" finial at the base and top of the tree.

Mark the branch locations at roughly equal intervals. You don't need the precision of dividers, but don't be random.

To make a V-cut with a 1" skew, use an underhand grip with your index finger hooked under the tool rest to anchor your hand.

Now skip two lines and cut a V-cut at the fourth line. Skip two more lines and make a V-cut at the seventh line, and continue in the sequence until you reach the top of the tree. Stop the lathe and have a look at the Vs to make sure they're cut cleanly.

For expediency, leave the V-cuts unsanded, as it's difficult to sand well with a constant air/wood transition. If you are compelled to sand the V-cuts, make a sanding aid by cutting a length of wood to a triangle the width of your V-cuts. With a spray adhesive, adhere sandpaper to the stick. Then use a back-and-forth motion to sand one side of the V. Flip the tool over and sand the other side.

Remount the ornament at another offset axis. Check again to make sure the ornament doesn't hit the tool rest. (Make sure you really did pick an unused axis, not the one you selected earlier.) Make a series of V-cuts at the second, fifth, and eighth lines until you again reach the top of the tree. Then remount the ornament on the last axis and cut on the remaining lines.

Add color

Remove the ornament from the lathe and set up a painting station. You'll need a clear sealer to keep the paint from wicking into unwanted areas. (Choose clear spray paint, spray lacquer, shellac, or sanding sealer.) Be sure to seal the walls of the V-cuts. Allow the sealer to dry.

After the sealer dries, paint the inside of the V-cuts with green acrylic paint. Neatness doesn't count as you'll be turning away excess paint. Allow the paint to dry.

Remount the ornament in your chuck. Bring up the tailstock for additional support. Use your skew to skim the tree to remove paint and pencil lines. Stop the lathe to make sure you've removed all marks and excess paint *(Photo 5)*.

Turn the angel

Reduce the finial area to the maximum diameter and height of the angel, leaving a nub for continued tailstock support. Use a 1/4" spindle gouge to turn her head and shoulders/wing tops. Undercut the wing/shoulder area about 1/32".

Use a 1/4" or 1/2" skew to make an undercut V-cut to define the bottom of the wing. Then turn the bottom of the angel's dress, blending it into the V-cut at the bottom of the wing. Turn a shallow cove with a spindle gouge to add some character to the wing *(Photo 6)*.

With a parting tool, reduce the trunk to final diameter (3/8" to 1/2"). Take a finishing cut on the trunk by using the parting tool like a skew, or use a small skew or spindle gouge. Clean up the bottom of the tree and the top of the base with a skew *(Photo 7)*.

Finishing details

Sand the ornament with progressively finer abrasives, starting with a grit appropriate for the surface your tooling left. With sanding out of the way, remove the nub at the head and sand the top of the head.

Use the tailstock to dimple the head to drill for hanger/halo mounting. Then use a #55 bit to drill the hanger mounting hole. (Jump ahead to creating the halo and make a sample so you can measure the appropriate drill diameter.)

If you're turning a batch of ornaments, save some time by mounting the drill in a pin chuck. Then instead of swapping out the tailstock for a drill chuck, back off the tailstock, mount the tail of the pin chuck on the tailstock, line up the drill point, and then advance the tailstock while holding the pin chuck in place by hand. Part the ornament off at the base. Use a drum or disc sander to sand the bottom of the base flat.

Skim the surface of the tree to remove excess paint and pencil lines.

Shape the side of the wing by cutting a shallow cove.

With a skew, clean up the surface of the trunk and base.

Pick whatever part of the ornament looks best to you as the front and use a drum sander to sand the front of the angel almost flat. Don't sand into the tree, and stop short of the halo mounting hole in her head.

Apply the finish of your choice (I prefer lacquer or clear gloss paint).

To make it easier to hold the ornament during spraying, I find bamboo skewers (available in kitchen shops) are ideal *(Photo 8)*. Measure the diameter of the skewer and use a drill of that diameter to drill a hole in the center of the base of the ornament.

Prepare a drying stand by drilling slightly larger holes in a scrap piece of wood—size the wood piece to accommodate all the ornaments in your batch.

Hold on to the skewer with one hand and spray the can of finish with the other. You can turn and angle the ornament with the skewer until the finish has been applied to the whole surface (even the bottom). Then set the skewer into the holder until the finish dries. Apply another coat if needed.

Angel needs a halo

Bend a halo/ornament hanger from wire. Select something smooth and round to match the desired diameter of the halo. (I use the shank of a 1/4" drill.)

Cut a short length (about 2") of 22-gauge brass wire and clamp both ends in a vise. Insert the rod into the loop and turn the rod until the wire is twisted into a tight spiral.

Unclamp the vise to remove the wire and slide the loop off the rod. Bend the spiraled wire so it angles below the center of the loop (Photo 9). At the point of the wire directly below the center of the loop, bend the spiral wire so it points straight down.

Trim the wire to length with wire cutters. Apply some cyanoacrylate (CA) glue to the tip of the spiral wire and insert the wire into the hole drilled in the angel's head. If you want to hang the now-finished ornament you can loop a hanger wire around the base of the halo.

Starting with the basic ornament you can make many changes, such as leaving off the base, changing or omitting paint, or changing the finial. Some of these are discussed in the Variations sidebar on my website.

Basement woodturner David Reed Smith (David@DavidReedSmith.com) lives in Hampstead, Maryland.

Using a bamboo skewer to hold the ornament, spray a clear finish to the tree.

To form a halo/ornament hanger, twist 22-gauge wire around the shank of a 1/4" drill.

Limited Penetration Tailstocks

Modified Point
Most commercially available tailstock centers are suboptimal for small work in soft wood because a cup center is too large and a point center tends to split the wood. One way to solve this problem is to shape your own center with a finer point and flat area to limit penetration.

Early Oneway live centers use a tapered dowel pin as the center pin. You can take the center to a well-stocked hardware store and find a tapered dowel pin that fits and has the amount of extension you want. Mount the new dowel pin in the tailstock and then mount the tailstock in your headstock. Find a rod or nail about the diameter of the tailstock knockout pin and insert it in the live center cross hole to

After filing a tapered dowel pin into a limited penetration center.

lock the tailstock. Tape the pin in place. Turn on the lathe at a slow speed and file the point however you like.

Newer Oneway tailstocks use a #0 Morse taper as the center pin. You can do the same thing if you can find a suitable pin. An Internet search convinced me it would be easier to make a pin. Chuck a 3/8" rod on your lathe and file until it matches the taper of the pin that came with the chuck. Then mount the new pin in the tailstock center and shape the point.

Washer
A V-point tailstock and a small washer provide a low-tech solution. If you get tired of chasing the washer across the shop, glue it in place with CA glue.

Use a small washer to prevent the tailstock from penetrating too far and splitting the soft pine.

Ring-Turned Trees

Roger Zimmermann

These inside-out trees are ring-turned, a technique that allows you to shape both the inside and outside of an object and easily make multiples. First, two flat disks are fastened together with the pattern set in a slot in the wood. After turning the inside profile, the disks can be glued together to turn the outside shape. Then the trees can be sliced from the ring like thin wedges of cake. With a little imagination you can use the technique to design bells and other holiday ornaments.

Make a pattern

Begin by drawing a full-size pattern on paper like the one shown in *Figure 1*. A thick-tipped marker works well to achieve the width for the outline of the tree. Strike a line of symmetry through the tree, dividing it in half; the two sides of the pattern do not have to be identical. Here, the tree leans a bit and the symmetry is off just enough to give the ornament a handmade character.

Glue the pattern to two pieces of thin wood whose edges are butted together but not glued. Align the line of symmetry with the seam between the two pieces of wood. When the

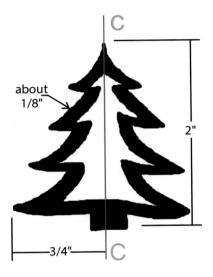

Figure 1. Use this as a model for your own tree design.

glue is dry, use a sharp knife to cut the paper pattern apart along the seam *(Photo 1)*.

With a bandsaw or scrollsaw, cut out each half pattern, both inside and outside edges *(Photo 2)*. Mark or paint the edges of the wood black.

Prepare two disks

Cut two disks of the wood you want to use for the ornaments. The larger the diameter, the greater the number of ornaments you can produce. I used two 9"- (230mm-) diameter pieces for these trees. Each one should be half the thickness of the full-size pattern.

Attach a glue block to one side of each disk. These blocks are tenons for mounting each disk into a scroll chuck. One at a time, mount each disk into the scroll chuck and

Glue the pattern to two thin pieces of wood, then slice down the middle to create half-trees.

Carefully cut out each pattern piece.

Make sure the face of each disk is flat, so they can later be glued together securely.

Screw the two disks together and carefully true up the assembly.

AW 28:5, p22

true up each face to make them flat (Photo 3). They will be glued together eventually, so ensure that each surface is flat.

Screw the two disks together using two screws, one on each side. If possible, orient the grain patterns on the disks to give what looks like branches sloping down. Make sure the screws are placed far enough on the inside of the disks, away from where the tree pattern will be turned. The glue blocks will be on the outsides (Photo 4).

Using one of the glue-block tenons, mount the assembly into the scroll chuck, using the tailstock center for support. Before tightening the chuck's jaws, ensure that the seam between the disks is perpendicular to the axis of the lathe. Re-center the piece as needed until the seam is aligned properly. Tighten the chuck jaws, and then true up the tailstock-end glue block. True up the disks. Everything should now be in alignment.

Insert the pattern
Take the screwed-together disks to the bandsaw and cut a slot for the patterns (Photo 5). You will need to use a board that is thicker than the glue-block tenon to support the disk when cutting the slot.

Remove the screws and separate the two disks. Glue one half of the pattern into each disk, making sure the edges along the symmetry line are flush with the faces of the disks, and that the bottom of the pattern is flush with the outside diameter of the disks (Photo 6).

Turn the inside profile
One at a time, mount each disk into a scroll chuck using the glue blocks. Support the disk with the tailstock. Remove material that represents the inside of the tree pattern until you just touch the painted edge of the pattern (Photo 7). I do not sand the

trees, but if you want yours smooth, now is the time to sand.

With the inside profiles turned on each disk, glue the disks together where the profiles come together. To ensure a good bond, apply a light coating of wood glue to both disks. Align the disks at the pattern slot and clamp them together. This completes the inside profile of the tree.

Turn the outside profiles
After the glue has set, remount the assembly, using the glue-block tenons, into a scroll chuck and turn the first outside profile. Use the same techniques as for the inside. Sand if you want. When the first side of the tree is complete, flip the assembly end for end and remount it to complete the other side.

The magic
Carefully part away the turned profile ring from the wood left on the inner area of the disk. Use a very slow lathe speed for the finishing cut that separates the tree-profile ring from the solid wood in the middle.

Now it is time to slice the ring into wedges to cut individual trees. Cut the wedges so the tree trunk is between 1/4" to 1/2" (6mm to 12mm) thick, or whatever looks about right to your eye (Photo 8). Real trees are thicker near their trunk, so the orientation of the tip of the tree to the inside of the ring results in an appropriately sculpted look.

Voilà! The tree appears like magic. A ring this size will make about forty inside-out trees.

Sand and finish the trees however you want. I happen to like the rough cut surfaces. To that, I apply tung oil or thinned acrylic paint. Happy holidays.

Roger Zimmerman is a retired engineer who has been turning for more than 35 years.

Cut a slot in the disks that will house the two tree-pattern pieces. (Avoid the screws.)

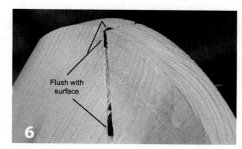

Flush with surface

Glue a half-pattern into the slot on each disk. The inside of each pattern should face the outside of the disk, away from the tenon. The trunk of the tree should be on the outside rim of the disk.

Turn the inside tree profile of each disk. The black paint on the pattern warns you when to stop.

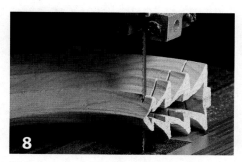

With the outside profiles turned and the center of the disk parted off, saw out the trees.

Easy-to-Turn Snowman

Nick Cook

With the holiday season upon us, many start thinking about handmade ornaments and decorations. The possibilities are endless: bells to trees, hollow vessels to miniature birdhouses, snowmen and everything in between. Some of my ornaments are very complicated, but this snowman is very simple. Almost anyone can make it with a little practice and patience. It is also an excellent project to help develop your skills with the skew.

Stock and weight

Weight is a major factor when making ornaments. In fact, the local "Festival of Trees" has restricted ornaments to a maximum of only 2-1/2 ounces. Choose your stock carefully or downsize the ornament to keep the weight down.

I have selected basswood for this snowman ornament. It is both light in weight and in color, so you won't have to paint it. Basswood is also very easy to turn as long as your tools are sharp. Walnut or most any other dark wood will work well for the top hat.

As a production item that I make to sell, I have found it more productive to make these snowmen two at a time between centers. It saves both time and material, even if you aren't going to sell them. Plus, you can't ever have too many ornaments. I start with 8/4 stock and cut it into squares approximately 1-3/4 x 1-3/4 in. Before cutting to length, I set the band saw table to

A flurry of traditional-style ornaments from the turner's shop. To speed production, Cook turns two snowmen at a time with the blank between centers.

45 degrees and saw the corners from the material. The resulting 8-sided or octagonal shapes are faster and easier to turn. With the band saw reset to square, I use a sliding table to cut the basswood stock to 8-in. lengths. The blanks are now ready to turn.

The walnut stock is prepared in the same manner. The final blanks should be about 1-1/2 in. square by 4 to 6 in. long. Smaller scraps and off-fall from other projects will work fine.

Turning the bodies

I use a 1/2-in. mini-spur drive and a cup-shaped live center to turn most small-to-medium-sized spindles. This is an ideal combination for these snowmen ornaments.

Mount the blank between centers and position the tool rest just below the centerline. It should be parallel to the stock and about 1/8 in. from the corners. Always rotate the stock by hand to ensure clearance all around before turning the lathe on.

Set the lathe speed at approximately 2000 RPM and start the machine. You can use a large spindle roughing gouge at first, if you like, but a large skew is a better choice. I prefer the 1-1/4 in. oval skew. Using this tool on a wood as soft as basswood is not only fun, but it also helps to build confidence and skill with the skew.

Rough turn the blank to a cylinder as large as you can keep it. Measure and mark the blank

Photos by Cathy Wike-Cook

AW 14:4, p14

to lay out the two snowmen. I use a marking gauge or layout tool for marking the three sections of each snowman. This tool is simple to make and will save a lot of time, especially if you are making multiples. I set the tool for the following dimensions: I leave the bottom of the ornament full diameter x 1-1/4 in. long; the middle section is about 1 in. dia. x 1/8 in. long, and the head is 3/4 in. dia. and 3/4 in. long.

The gauge is made from a small piece of scrap lumber approximately 10 in. long and 2-to-3 in. wide. Measure and mark the gauge where you will make cuts in the turning blank. Use small brads nailed into the edge of the gauge and cut off the heads with wire cutters to leave sharp ends on the brads. You may need to tap the ends of the brads to make them the same length for marking the blank. You are ready to mark the basswood blank.

I use a 3/8-in. bedan tool to cut about half way through the material at the center of the blank to separate the two ornaments. With layout lines in place, I use either the 3/8-in. bedan or 3/8-in. parting tool with a turning gate attached to rough down the center section of each snowman to approximately 1-1/8 in. Next turn down the outer ends of each to 3/4 in. dia. You can use a separate parting tool with another turning gate or just use the same one and turn down past the gate to approximately 3/4 in. You should now have two halves cut to three different diameters each.

Now comes the fun part, turning the three segments into beads. This is where you learn to use the skew. I prefer the 3/8-in. round skew for this, but most any style of skew will work. The round profile makes rolling a bead very easy. First take the long point of the skew and cut straight down the side of each

After the snowmen are sawn apart, angle the top of each on the disk sander so the hat will sit at a festive angle.

segment. Then make a second cut at each point to produce half of a V. This will give you room to roll each of the beads. You may or may not want to mark the center of each bead with a pencil line. This can help in making each of the beads uniform.

Lay the flat of the bevel on the centerline and roll the skew in each direction to produce a well-rounded bead on each segment. Take care not to get in a hurry. Several light cuts work much better than trying to take it in one heavy cut. It will also help in building your confidence.

Once all six beads have been turned and the intersections are crisp Vs, you are ready to sand the surface. Clean cuts on basswood should allow you to sand with 180- or 220-grit sandpaper. Anything heavier will leave scratches. Use a small parting tool to cut down each end of the blank and at the center. Remove the blank from the lathe and finish cutting with the band saw or a handsaw. With the two ornaments separated, you can now sand the ends of each. Use a belt or disk sander with 60- or 80-grit sandpaper to sand the bottom of each piece flat. Sand

the top or head of each snowman at a slight angle to make his hat tip to one side.

Turning the top hat
Place the walnut blank in a scroll chuck. Use a skew or gouge to rough the blank to a cylinder approximately 1 in. dia. Trim the exposed end of the blank to a slight dome with a skew or small spindle gouge. Measure back about 1 in. and make a parting cut with a thin parting tool about half way through the blank. Use a small skew to shape the top hat and brim. Sand with 180-grit sandpaper and part off the top hat. Use the belt or disk sander to make the bottom of the hat flat. The hat is ready to attach to the basswood snowman. Use a drop or two of cyanoacrylate glue and carefully center the hat on the head of the snowman. It is now ready for the finishing touches.

Finishing the ornament
Once assembled, spray the ornament with a clear sanding sealer before applying any other decoration. This will keep any additional finish from

The author can turn a series of hats from a single block held in a chuck. Here he prepares to catch a hat as he slices it free.

bleeding into the wood. Next I add the scarf. I use 1/8-in. or 3/16-in. satin ribbon available from most any fabric or craft supply store. I like dark green and red. I cut it into lengths of about 4 in. to 5 in. to make it easier to tie and handle. Any shorter and it is almost impossible to work with. I tie the ribbon around the neck of the snowman and put a drop of CA glue on the knot to keep it from coming apart. I then cut off the excess ribbon with scissors and tack the ends down with tacky glue, which also is available in fabric and craft stores. Apply it to the ribbon with the end of a toothpick to avoid getting too much. Allow the tacky glue to set before proceeding.

After the tacky glue is dry, you may now work on the buttons, eyes, nose and mouth. I use puffy Puff paint for all but the mouth. It too is available in fabric and craft stores in most any color. It is polymer paint and comes in an applicator bottle. Simply cut the tip and it is ready to apply. Squeeze the bottle with tip at the point you wish to leave a dot and pull the tip up from the surface. It will leave a small lump of paint. Black works well for eyes, buttons and even the nose if you like. Orange is a good choice if you want the nose to look like a carrot. You can use the same paint to decorate wine stoppers and other projects.

For the mouth, I use an indelible fine-tip magic marker such as the Sharpie. Four or five dots in an arch gives the snowman a big smile. Put the ornaments aside to dry before proceeding. After the paint has dried, I apply a coat of clear satin lacquer to seal the final product.

The only thing left is a screw eye for hanging the ornament. I use tiny silver or brass colored eyes. I drill a pilot hole at the drill press to make sure it goes in straight. Make sure you center the hole on the body of the ornament and not the top hat since it is at an angle. This would cause the ornament to hang at an angle. These make great stocking stuffers, tree ornaments or decorations of holiday packages. Happy Holidays.

Nick Cook is a writer, teacher and professional turner in Marietta, GA.

Buttons, eyes, nose and mouth are created with polymer puffy paint, which dries proud of the surface. Other accents can be added with permanent markers.

An Icicle Snowman

Nick Cook

Christmas tree ornaments are always a good item to make and sell. This one is quite simple. There is no hollowing, no thin spindle and no assembly required. This is nothing more than a simple spindle with a little detail. It is an icicle snowman. Everyone will love it.

Size does not matter; weight, however, does. The local Festival of Trees restricts weight to a maximum of 2-1/2 ounces. You may need to invest in a set of postal scales to stay within the limits, if you plan to donate your ornaments to a charity such as this.

My favorite material for making the icicle snowman ornament is hard maple. I like the wood's bright, light color and its tight grain cuts and finishes with ease. I have also used soft maple, ash, oak and cherry. I like to start with 5/4 stock and cut it into squares roughly 1x1x8 in. The proportions work out well for this size and it is a great way to use scraps from around the shop. You can, however, make them all different sizes and use a variety of woods.

Once the blanks are cut to size, I locate and mark the center on each end. I use a spring-loaded or automatic center punch, which leaves a dimple in each end of the blank. This makes it easy to position the workpiece between centers on the lathe.

Hone your turning skills and spread a little holiday cheer with these icicle holiday ornaments.

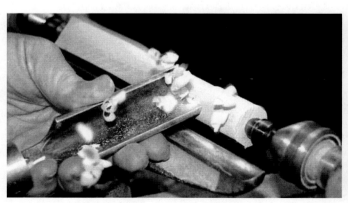

The 1-1/4 in. spindle roughing gouge quickly reduces the blank to a smooth cylinder.

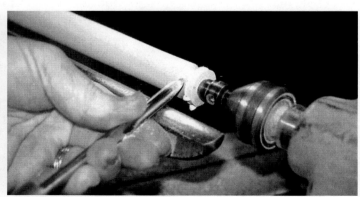

Most of the detail can be shaped using a 3/8 in. spindle gouge.

Photos by Cathy Wike-Cook

AW 17:4, p41

Begin shaping the icicle with the hat. The toolrest is mounted slightly below center, and the top of the icicle is secured by the tailstock.

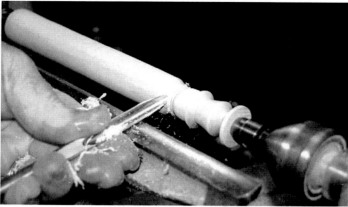

After establishing the hat brim, the author shapes the head of the snowman, taking care to make the round head looks as if it fits naturally into the hat.

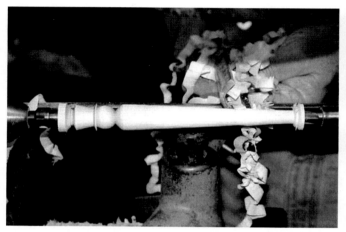

Using a gouge or a skew, taper the body from the top of the icicle (tailstock end) to the base, which is mounted at the headstock end with a mini-drive center.

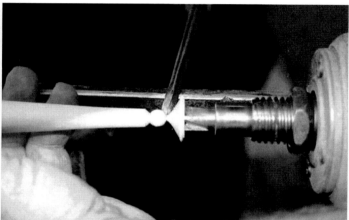

After shaping a sphere at the bottom of the ornament, the author reaches over the work to steady the piece as he separates it from the lathe.

Time to turn

I prefer a 1/2-in. diameter mini-spur drive-center for most work up to about 4 in. diameter. Rude Osolnik introduced me to the mini-spur more than 25 years ago. His first one was fashioned from an old cup-style dead center. He used a file to create teeth on the ring or cup. Then he extended and sharpened the center point. This allowed him to mount spindles, including his signature candlesticks, without stopping his lathe. He very graphically pointed out to me how much time I was wasting by stopping and starting the machine as I was turning baby rattles.

Mount the blank and position the tool rest just below center. Set the lathe speed at approximately 3000 rpm. Start the machine. I begin with a 1-1/4 in. spindle roughing gouge and turn the blank down to a cylinder.

I use a 3/8 in. spindle gouge with a long fingernail grind (about 25° bevel) for detailing. I start at the tailstock end and work back towards the headstock. The first cut defines the top of the hat. The next cut sets the brim so you can finish shaping the rest of the top hat. The brim should be thin, approximately 1/16-in. A bead or small sphere is turned just under the brim of the hat to create the snowman's head. Make the diameter of the bead a little larger on the top (where it meets the hat) than at the bottom (where it meets the icicle body). Think of the top of the bead ending somewhere under the hat. Otherwise the hat may look as if it's perched too high on the snowman's head.

The body or icicle is next. You can use either the roughing gouge or a skew to taper the rest of the blank down to approximately 5/16 in. diameter. I add a small ball or sphere at the bottom of the icicle to finish it off. I sand the piece with 150-grit and then 220-grit. Then, I use a piece of 1/8 in. thick tempered Masonite to burn a band into the top hat just above the brim.

Turn each end of your snowman down to just under 1/8 in. diameter.

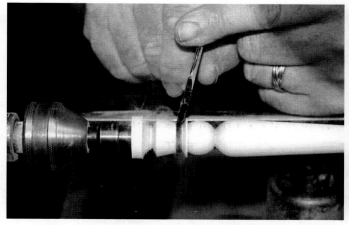

Create the dark hat band by pressing a piece of Masonite against the spinning wood.

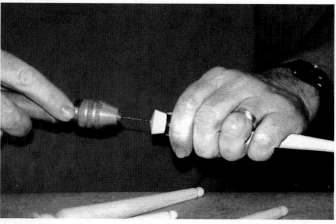

Be sure to predrill the hole for the slender eye hooks, using a drill in a pin vise or a Dremel-type rotary tool.

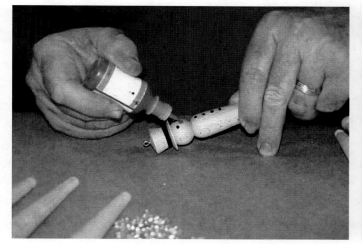

Form the button eyes with thick polymer puff paint, and draw the mouth with a black Sharpie-type pen.

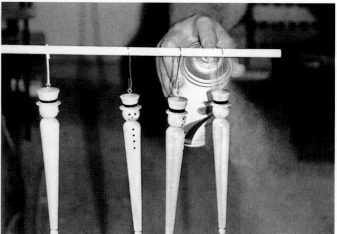

Finish the ornaments by spraying them with two or three coats of Deft lacquer. Deft also can be brushed on.

You should always separate the workpiece from the tailstock end first and then from the headstock end. Once separated, you will need to touch up each end with a little sandpaper.

Use a small drill bit, about 1/16 in. diameter, to drill a pilot hole in the center of the top hat using a Dremel tool, flex-shaft, or pin vise to hold the drill bit. I use #217-1/2 screw eyes, available from many craft suppliers and hardware stores. If you don't predrill pilot holes, the eyes probably will twist off the slender screws.

Ready to finish

I use puff paint for the finishing touches. This is a thick, polymer paint that is three-dimensional when applied to most surfaces. It is available from most fabric and craft supply outlets. The eyes and buttons are done in black and the nose is orange. You can add a little extra orange paint to pull the nose up into a carrot shape.

I use a fine-tip Sharpie pen to make dots for the mouth. You can also use ribbon to create a scarf around the snowman's neck. If you have plenty of time, you could insert small twigs into the body to create arms.

Once all the details are in place and dry, I spray on a coat or two of clear lacquer for a final finish. These ornaments make great gifts or decorations on presents. Make lots of them and give them away to friends and family. It is an excellent project to help improve your woodturning skills.

Happy Holidays.

Nick Cook is a professional turner, teacher, and writer in Marietta, GA.

The Icicle Ornament

Bob Rosand

For many years, turned Christmas ornaments have been a mainstay of my turning. When the sales of other work are slow, I always manage to sell an ornament or two. I have also had the opportunity to demonstrate my ornaments for numerous AAW chapters and at various regional and national events.

It always surprises me a bit that people want to see my ornaments turned time after time. I'll show you the basic procedure for making a light-weight icicle ornament with a hollow globe, along with some variations on the theme that my wife, Susan, and I have come up with over the years.

Materials and tools

To make this ornament, I suggest a 2-1/2" x 1-3/4" piece of figured burl that will become the globe. To turn the icicle and the finial, you will need a piece of straight-grained wood about 1-1/4" square by 7-1/2" long. I prefer to turn the globe from a light-colored wood like oak, ash, or cherry because the lighter woods don't get "lost" when the ornament hangs on a tree bough.

You also will need a good chuck with #2 jaws for turning the globe. The Talon chuck by Oneway is ideal for this because of its small size, but other chucks will do just fine. A set of spigot jaws is almost indispensable for turning the icicle, but you can manage without them— the process is just a bit slower.

AW 19:3, p28

The icicle requires a small roughing-out gouge. A 3/4" roughing-out gouge works fine, but if you turn a lot of these ornaments, a 1/2" roughing-out gouge is a big help. You also will need some good bent-angle tools for hollowing the globe and a small skew. Other than that, standard turning tools should suffice: 3/8" spindle gouge, 1/2" spindle gouge (optional), mini square-nosed scraper, small (1/4") round-nosed scraper, small skew, parting tool.

Turn the globe

Glue the burl to a waste block, which is held in the #2 jaws of your chuck. Next, turn the globe to a finished diameter of about 2-1/4". Shape the globe with a 3/8" spindle gouge as shown in *Photo A*. I prefer a "flat" globe on the top and bottom rather than a round globe. This allows for an easier fit of the icicle and finial, since both have to be undercut to fit on the globe.

Be sure to make the glue block from a hard wood like oak or maple—not plywood or pine. The reason for this is important: The plys in the plywood may separate. Additionally, pine is too soft and may pull out of the jaws, especially if you have a catch.

As you shape the globe to the final dimensions, make sure that you leave enough material at the top of the globe to allow for hollowing, but remove enough material so that you can see what the final shape will be.

Once you have the globe turned, drill a 3/8" hole through the entire ornament into the waste block as shown in *Photo B*. Then use a small square-nosed scraper to open the hole in the bottom of the ornament to about 3/4" wide; this allows room to hollow. Now use the bent angle tools to hollow the interior of the ornament. I prefer a combination of the bent-angle tools and a small round-nosed scraper to hollow the interior as shown in *Photo C*. Hollow the wall thickness to about 1/8". You don't have to worry about extreme thinness here—the idea is to remove some of the interior mass so that

the finished ornament does not weigh down the pine bough. As you become more proficient, you can turn thinner walls.

As you turn, clean out the shavings; if they build up too much, they can grab the tool and destroy the globe. (The shavings build up more with green wood than dry wood.) Compressed air is one solution, but if you don't have a compressor, a small piece of plastic hose or straw will suffice to blow out the shavings.

After turning the interior, use the spindle gouge to continue refining the shape of the globe. Don't forget that you have a 3/8" hole drilled through the entire globe. When you are satisfied with the shape of your ornament, sand the globe, apply sanding sealer, and part it from the lathe as shown in *Photo D*.

Turn the icicle

Place the icicle stock in the spigot jaws of your chuck. The length of the spigot jaws are about 1-1/2", so

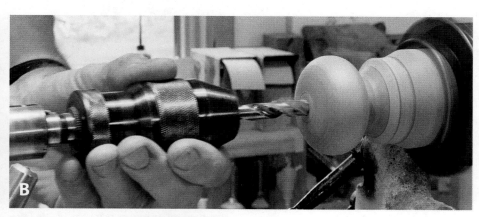

they hold the icicle well as shown in *Photo E*.

If you don't have a set of spigot jaws, consider drilling a 1" hole in a waste block, then turn a 1" tenon on the icicle stock and glue the two pieces. Although this takes longer to prepare, it's cheaper than buying spigot jaws.

Next, use the roughing-out gouge to start turning the icicle. You won't have the support of the tailstock to rely on, so take light cuts. I turn the smallest segment first (the tip of the icicle). I reduce the diameter with the roughing-out gouge, then refine the shape with a small skew and small spindle gouge as shown in *Photo F*.

This first segment defines the rest of the icicle segments. Each successive one must be a bit larger and longer than the previous one. As you finish a segment, sand, apply sanding sealer and then turn the next one. I usually turn four segments followed by a cove and some other decorative cuts at the top of the icicle.

When you are satisfied with the icicle, turn a tenon with your parting tool that will fit into the large hole in the bottom of the globe as shown in *Photo G*.

Once I have the tenon sized to fit the hole in the bottom of the globe (about 3/4"), I use a small parting tool ground at an angle or a skew to undercut the icicle so that its shoulder fits nicely into the globe and there are no gaps.

Finally, glue the icicle into the body of the ornament.

The finial
Turn the finial from the remainder of the icicle stock.

I first turn a 3/8" tenon on that stock and then undercut it with the skew or small parting tool. Be sure to check the fit. I then refine the shape, part it from the lathe, reverse the

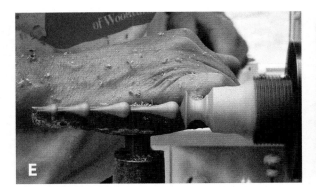
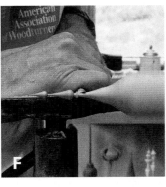
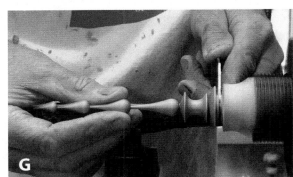

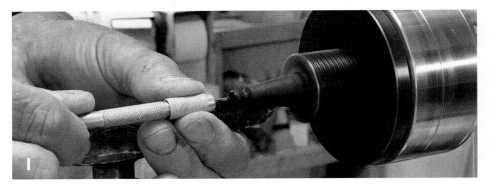

finial and hold it in the spigot jaws. This allows me to make any final changes on the finial and also drill a 1/8"-diameter hole as shown in *Photo H* to accept a small ebony knob (a nice decorative touch).

I then drill another small hole with a pin vise in the ebony knob to accept a screw eye for hanging the ornament as shown in *Photo I*. Screw eyes (#18A is an ideal size) run about 10 cents apiece. If you want to save some money, consider using cut-off fishing hooks or glue in nylon filament.

For final steps, glue the finial in place, and spray the ornament with satin lacquer.

If you are just starting out with Christmas tree ornaments, you might consider experimenting with icicles that are somewhat shorter than the length suggested in this article. As you gain confidence and skill, you will be able to lengthen the icicles.

Bob Rosand is a professional turner and educator living in Bloomsburg, PA. He has been a frequent contributor to the AW Journal.

Variations on a theme

Now that you have the basic ornament down pat, you may be looking for ways to vary the design. Over the years, I have found this to be a necessity, particularly selling ornaments at craft shows. I have lost more than one sale by not having this years "new and improved" model. For me, the basic globe and icicle stay the same, but here are some variations that you may consider.

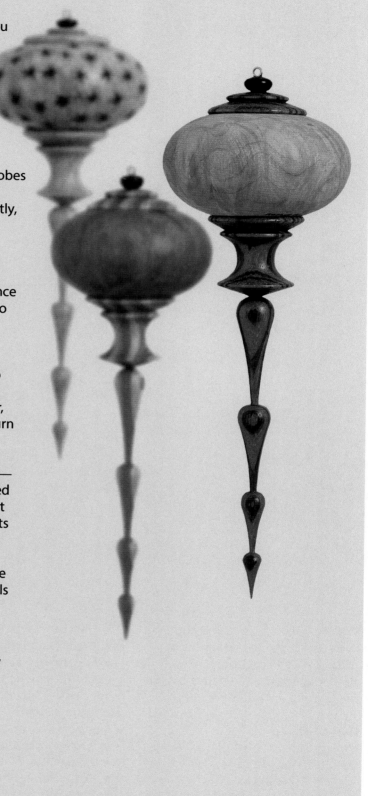

1. Paint the globe. Susan grabs a handful of the globes that I turn and paints winter country scenes on some of them and holly leaves on others. Recently, she has been experimenting with painting fall leaves on some globes.

2. Marbleize the globe. We experimented with marbleizing a few years ago, which sold well. Since paint covers the globe, marbleizing allows you to use less expensive wood.

3. Turn the globe from banksia seedpods. I'm not particularly fond of turning banksia, since it is so dirty, but the ornaments turned from it sell well. I usually turn the walls of the globes a bit thicker, since the banksia "eyes" tend to pop out if you turn it too thin.

4. Bleach the globe. I prefer two-part wood bleach—not household bleach. At first I was not impressed with the idea of bleaching the globes—I thought that character would be lost. Bleached ornaments are now one of my favorite variations.

5. Dye the globes. Some of my ornament globes are dyed with red aniline dye and the icicle and finials are turned of red-and-white striped color wood.

6. Woodburn the globe. I have recently added pyrography skills. I now burn stars on the globes, which produces a totally different effect. This technique sells well.

7. Laminate the globe. Consider gluing up some of those precious scraps that you just can't bear to throw away and turning them into ornament globes.

Twisted Icicles

Bill Bowers

Turning Christmas ornaments is a fun-filled fall project. Here's a variation that adds the challenge of a double-barley twist to the popular icicle design.

Get started

For lathe tools, you will need a 1-1/4" spindle roughing gouge, 1/8" parting tool, 3/8" spindle gouge or 1/2" skew chisel, and 1/4"-square scraper. To hollow out the globe, use a small bent- or curved-angle hollow tool.

The twists on the icicle require a lathe index system or an externally applied index system. You'll also need a 7/8" cup drive, a 4-jaw scroll chuck with 2"-deep jaws, a 4-jaw scroll chuck with 1" jaws for small-diameter work, and a Jacobs chuck.

For detail on the captured ring, a curved dental pick is ideal. (The next time you visit your dentist, ask the hygienist for worn-out dental picks—they make great mini tools for projects like this.)

To cut the icicle twists, you'll need a 1/16" tungsten carbide rasp; Dixie Industrial Supply (dixiepins.com) is one source of 80-grit rasps.

For turning stock, select 3×3×6" stock for the globe. I turned several globes from the seasoned trunk of my family's Christmas tree from the previous year. Select the trunk area where many branches exit, and then bandsaw a 6" segment to be turned between centers. The icicle requires

AW 21:4, p20

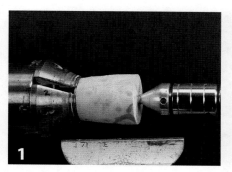

1 With a spindle roughing gouge, turn the globe stock to about a 2-1/2" diameter.

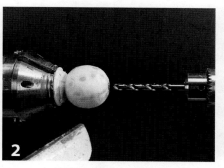

2 Mount a 3/8" brad-point bit in a Jacobs chuck, then drill through the globe.

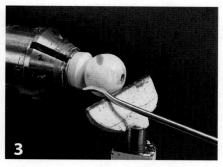

3 With micro hollowing tools, reduce the globe wall thickness to 1/8".

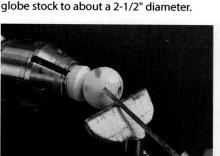

4 With a 1/4"-square scraper, square the opening of the globe bottom.

5 After turning the stock round, reduce the icicle diameter at the headstock to 9/16".

6 With a thin parting tool, reduce the icicle diameter to fit the globe's bottom opening.

7 For a captive ring, use a cove cut to create the center band.

1×1×6-1/2" stock in a contrasting species. For this project, I used Honduran redheart, which turns easily and details well.

When turning the globe, wear a face shield and a throw-away shirt, as a lot of pine sap will stick to your clothing and tools.

Turn the globe

Mount the 3×3×6" turning stock in spigot jaws at one end. Then, bring up the tailstock. With a 1-1/4" spindle roughing gouge, turn the stock round. Note the pleasant appearance of the numerous branch knots as shown in *Photo 1*.

Turn a 2-1/2"-diameter sphere, being sure to leave enough stock near the spigot jaws to support drilling. Mount a Jacobs chuck and 3/8" brad-point bit in your tailstock. After dialing down the lathe speed to about 200 rpm, drill through the sphere as shown in *Photo 2*.

Using small hollowing tools, as shown in *Photo 3*, reduce the interior of the globe to about 1/8" thick. Use compressed air to frequently remove small chips from the interior of the globe.

Check the wall thickness with a feeler gauge bent from a coat hanger. Then clean up and square the globe opening with a 1/4"-square scraper, as shown in *Photo 4*.

With a parting tool, bring up the tailstock and reduce the tenon to about 5/8" diameter. Sand the sphere with progressively finer grits, moving from 180 grit to 400 grit. With a 1/8" parting tool, part off the globe.

Turn the icicle

Mount the icicle stock between centers and turn the stock round. With a skew, turn a slight taper at the tailstock. At the headstock, turn the dowel to about a 9/16" diameter to fit #1 Talon or comparable jaws, as shown in *Photo 5*.

With calipers, measure the globe's largest opening. Then use a

parting tool to turn a matching spigot about 1-1/2" from the end stock, as shown in *Photo 6*.

Use a 3/8" spindle gouge to turn a cove as shown in *Photo 7*. Leave a 3/32" rim for what will become the captive ring.

With a sharpened dental pick, round over the ring, slightly undercutting the ring on each side, as shown in *Photo 8*.

Delicately sand the ring with 180- to 400-grit sandpaper, as shown in *Photo 9*. Before sanding, apply stick wax to your sandpaper. The

A used dental pick (sharpened with a hook) is ideal for undercutting the captive ring.

After sanding the captive ring, part off the ring with the dental tool.

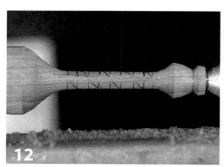

Lay out the two cut lines for the right-handed double-barley twist.

Before parting off the captive ring, smooth the surfaces with wax-loaded sandpaper.

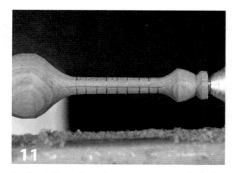

At the tailstock end, lay out start and pitch lines for the double-barley twist.

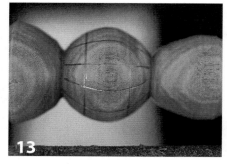

Lay out 12 horizontal start lines and two circumferential pitch lines.

wax will act as a lubricant, cooling agent, dust suppressant, and sanding sealer for non-oil finishes.

Part off the ring with the dental tool, as shown in *Photo 10*.

Add the twists

Shape the remainder of the icicle at the tailstock end. Lay out a thin double-barley twist as shown in *Photo 11*. On a 24-point lathe index system, mark horizontal pencil lines with the tool rest dead center at 6, 12, 18, and 24. These are the start lines. Next, mark circumferential

lines every 4 mm, then divide the spaces in half. These are the pitch (degree of slope steepness) lines. For a right-handed twist, start at the tailstock end and draw a diagonal pencil line from the lower right-hand corner to the upper left-hand corner of the rec-tangle. Follow sequentially into the adjacent forward rectangle until you reach the headstock.

Skip a rectangle at the tailstock end and draw another line yielding two cut lines, as shown in *Photo 12*. Next, draw the layout for spirals on the sphere. Spirals that are about

25–33 percent of the circumference are most appealing. To give a smooth curve to the surface of the sphere, space pitches narrower at the poles.

Mark 12 equidistant horizontal lines utilizing the 24-point index on the lathe. Then add two pitch lines, one at the Tropic of Cancer and one at the Tropic of Capricorn, as shown in *Photo 13*.

Starting at the headstock end, draw a pencil line from the lower left-hand corner of one trapezoid to the upper right-hand corner. Continue the pencil line into the

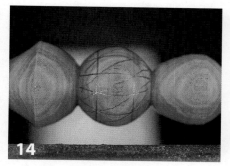

14 The section of the sphere shows 12 cut lines for a left-handed twist.

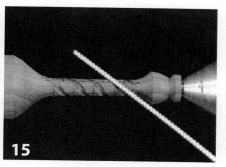

15 With a 1/16" rasp, cut the coves for the barley twist. Between cuts, lock the lathe spindle.

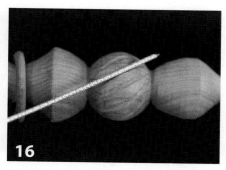

16 Use the rasp and lathe index to cut the 12 coves on the sphere.

17 Use ropes of twisted sandpaper to smooth the twists in the icicles.

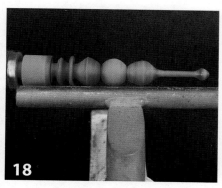

18 Turn a delicate ball on the tip of the icicle. Sand the tip carefully.

19 With the lathe running at about 200 rpm, thread the screweye into the ornament cap.

next trapezoid until you reach the tailstock end. Do the same for the other 11 trapezoids to yield 12 left-handed cut lines, as shown in *Photo 14*.

Cut the twist lines with a 1/16" rasp, as shown in *Photo 15*. Lock the spindle and carefully rasp one twist, unlock the spindle, rotate the icicle, and continue the cuts. Remember to use a delicate touch on this thin, fragile icicle.

Use the same technique to rasp the 12 cut lines on the sphere as shown in *Photo 16*.

After establishing all the cut lines, sand the grooves with sandpaper twisted into 1/16" ropes, as shown in *Photo 17*. For a smooth appearance, use 80, 120, 150, 240, and 320 grits on all surfaces of the cut coves. Sand with a delicate hand. Use waxed sandpaper for a final sanding of the icicle. (Because wax will clog the coves, avoid applying

on the twists.) Be sure to remove all pencil marks.

After the sanding is complete, fashion the icicle tip, as shown in *Photo 18*, and sand it carefully. Part off the icicle. Verify the fit between the sphere and globe, then join the two pieces with thick cyanoacrylate (CA) glue.

Turn the ornament cap

With calipers, measure the diameter of the opening in the globe top. Turn a tenon to the diameter of the opening, then shape the cap. Sand through the grits listed earlier.

With a 1/16" bit, drill a small hole for a brass eyelet. Dial down the lathe speed to about 200 rpm and allow the lathe to turn the eyelet into the cap, as shown in *Photo 19*. With CA glue, adhere the cap to the globe.

Apply a finish of your choice, being careful to avoid drips around the captured ring. On these turned

ornaments, most buyers prefer a gloss finish over a satin finish.

Bill Bowers lives in Anchorage and is a member of the Alaskan Woodturners Association.

Sea Urchin Ornament

David Lutrick

Bob Rosand introduced turners to the exquisite beauty and detail of sea urchin shells. I have made over fifty such ornaments, and along the way I have figured out how to make them less fragile. The modifications strengthen the ornaments by adding internal rigid foam and eliminating the glue joints between the shell, icicle, and finial.

First modification

The first modification is to inject aerosol foam insulation into the shells prior to beginning the construction. The foam insulation adds significant strength to the shells, but insignificant weight. I can now handle the shells during construction as if they were made of wood. I have even dropped several completed ornaments from bench-top height to the floor without damage.

The aerosol foam insulation is the type sold for filling voids in walls. Sold in home improvement stores, it is made by Dow, DAP, and Owens Corning, among others. Choose one that has good dimensional stability, because some of the foams are sensitive to changes in relative humidity and temperature. Make sure the can comes with an extension tube or straw. Several cautions are worth noting. The foam is *extremely* sticky. Once dry, it can only be removed mechanically by picking or scraping off the residue. This applies to your hands as well as to the shells, so you might want to wear nitrile gloves. The foam is soluble in acetone before it cures, so keep a supply of acetone and a brush handy. After use, flush the straw and the top nozzle of the can with acetone before the foam solidifies.

If the top of the shell has an open hole, seal it by applying painter's tape on the outside of the hole or by placing a disk of tissue paper on the inside before injecting the foam into the bottom hole.

The foam expands slowly to about twice the wet volume before solidifying in approximately two hours. The correct amount of foam is difficult to control, because the amount released when pressing the aerosol can valve is somewhat unpredictable. *Photo 1* shows that using too much foam to fill a shell will result in a plume of excess foam; however, the excess can easily be removed by twisting it off or cutting it with a fine-toothed hobby saw after it is dry.

The expanding foam can split very fragile or thin shells, common for the purple and pink varieties, even if the foam can vent freely from the bottom hole in the shell. The splits will be along natural weak points in the shells, which may be hard to see.

Once the foam is dry and any excess is removed, proceed with the ornament construction.

Second modification

The second modification is to use a connecting center dowel between the icicle and the finial rather than gluing these pieces to the shell itself or making a close-fitting insert.

First, use a conical, spherical, or tapered grinding stone, about 1" in diameter, to form a smooth, beveled recess around the natural hole in the bottom of the shell *(Photos 2 and 3)*. This recess will be used to accept a matching-beveled base on the icicle. Just press the rotating stone, mounted into a power hand drill, into the hole far enough so that any irregular edges or shell spikes are ground away. The foam will be removed as well, but it provides

AW 24:3, p34

Excess foam can be removed by twisting it off or cutting it with a fine-toothed hobby saw.

Use a grinding stone to form a smooth, beveled recess around the natural hole in the bottom of the shell.

This recess will be used to accept a matching-beveled base on the icicle.

some strength to the shell during the grinding. I have experienced very little chipping while grinding the beveled hole. If the shell has a large hole in the top, as is common with the Sputnik variety, you may want to grind a recess for the finial base around that hole too.

The second step is to make the icicle. The icicle base needs to be turned to match the ground-out hole in the bottom of the shell. For some shell varieties, such as the Sputnik and pink sea urchin, you will probably need to turn a relatively large, beveled flange on the icicle base to cover the hole. On green and purple shells, a smaller, spherical base can be used.

Drill a hole for the connecting dowel in the icicle about 1/4" deep, just enough to get a good glue joint. You can do this step on the lathe or drill before mounting the wood on the lathe. You may use 1/4"- or 3/16"-diameter dowels, so drill your hole accordingly. *Photo 4* shows how the icicle, finial, and dowel are connected to the body of the sea urchin.

Construct the finial with a center hole to accept the dowel and design its base to match the top of the shell. On varieties that have a small top hole in a convex surface, undercut the base around the dowel hole. On varieties that have a larger hole, turn a beveled base to fit snugly into the top hole.

Complete the icicle and finial by sanding, polishing, and buffing, as desired.

Hanging the ornament

I use monofilament fishing line to hang the ornaments. This requires a third step, drilling a small-diameter hole through the finial in the axial direction. I do that on the lathe immediately after the dowel hole is drilled in the finial. The small-diameter drill bit tends to wander off the centerline, so take care or the hole will not be centered in the finial.

When the foam-filled shell, icicle, and finial are completed, glue a dowel in the icicle base that is long enough to go through the shell plus at least 1/2". To make a hole in the foam, use a rat-tail file. If the shell you are using does not have a hole in the top, you will need to file through the shell as well. Make the hole just big enough for the dowel. Insert the dowel, seating the icicle base in the beveled, bottom hole.

Carefully estimate the dowel length to ensure a snug fit between the shell and the finial. There should be enough dowel inserted into the

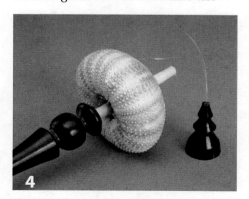

The icicle, finial, and dowel are connected to each other, through the body of the sea urchin.

finial hole for a good glue joint. If a beveled flange is also used for the top hole, both flanges should fit snugly inside their shell holes. If you will be using a monofilament hanger, make a loop of line and tie a small glass bead on the line before knotting it before gluing the assembly together. Place this on the inside of the finial. The bead and knot will jam in the finial hole and prevent the line from pulling out.

Dry fit the finial, with line inserted, on the dowel and adjust the length of the dowel if necessary. With the line loop in the finial and threaded through the top, glue the finial onto the dowel, pushing it down snugly on the shell.

With this construction, the weight of the ornament, icicle, and finial is borne primarily by the joined wooden components rather than the shell. The use of a grinding stone to bevel the holes, as well as turning a matching flange, eliminates the need to cut close-tolerance inserts and holes for glue joints.

To ship completed ornaments successfully, use a 3"-diameter cardboard mailing tube, cut to adequate length. Wrap the ornament in small-bubble, bubble wrap and place it in the mailing tube. The combination is light enough that even using postal letter rates is economical.

David Lutrick lives in Issaquah, WA.

Tree Topper

Bob Rosand

If you are a woodturner who turns holiday tree ornaments, the fall and early winter months are busy times. Over the years, I have turned a lot of tree ornaments, birdhouse ornaments, acorn birdhouse ornaments, teacher's bell ornaments. You name it; I've probably turned it for the holiday tree.

I wish I had a dollar for every time my wife, Susan, has asked me to come up with a design for a Christmas tree topper. But I just hadn't found a style of tree topper that I liked.

Then I remembered listening to someone critiquing hollow forms. That person (David Ellsworth, I recall) said that one of the characteristics of a good turned piece is that the form looks pleasing even if you turn it upside down. I turned one of my standard Christmas ornaments upside down and had my tree topper design right in front of me!

The major difference between the tree topper and the Christmas tree ornament that I turn—besides being upside-down—is that it's a bit larger, so that it noticeably crowns the top of a tree. And, this design has what I call a funnel on the bottom so it can fit securely on top of the tree.

The diameter of my Christmas tree ornaments is about 2-1/4". The tree topper globes are generally 2-1/2" or larger in diameter. The important thing is that the finial and funnel are all in proportion to the size of the globe.

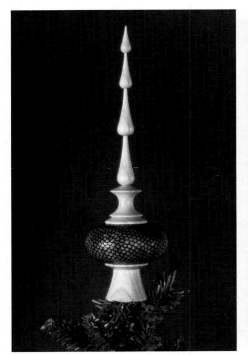

AW 20:3, p28

Get started

The finial requires a small spindle roughing gouge. A 3/4" spindle roughing gouge works fine, but if you like turning pieces like this, a 1/2" spindle roughing gouge is a big help.

You also will need some good bent-angle tools for hollowing the globe and a small round skew as shown in the drawing. Other than that, standard turning tools should suffice: 3/8" spindle gouge, 1/2" spindle gouge (optional), small squarenose scraper, 1/4" roundnose scraper, small skew, and parting tools.

You will need a sturdy chuck with #2 jaws for turning the globe. A set of spigot jaws is almost indispensable for turning the finial, but you can manage without them— the process is just a bit slower. If you don't have spigot jaws, use a

Photos: Bob Rosand

After truing up the globe stock, use calipers to check the diameter of the material. The globe should be about 2-1/2" in diameter.

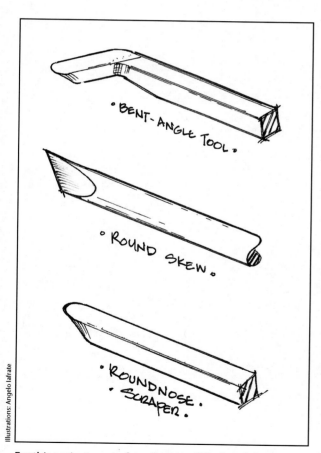

Illustrations: Angelo Iafrate

- BENT-ANGLE TOOL.
- ROUND SKEW.
- ROUNDNOSE. SCRAPER.

For this project, a set of small tools will be helpful. You may find use for as many as three bent-angle tools of various sizes to remove stock.

faceplate with an attached waste block. Drill a 1" hole in the waste block, then turn a 1" tenon.

In my work, I make extensive use of glue blocks. These allow me to use smaller pieces of precious wood and to get the wood away from the spinning jaws so that I can turn it safely. Don't allow the waste blocks to be too long, or you will have a chatter problem.

You will need a piece of burl about 2-3/4 × 2-1/2" for the tree-topper globe. If you have other nicely figured woods such as ambrosia maple, incorporate that.

You also will need a piece of straight-grained wood for the finial and a piece of similar wood for the funnel. For the toppers featured in this article, the finial material is about 1-3/8 × 8" and the funnel material about 1-3/8 × 4".

Turn the globe

Using a spindle gouge, true the globe stock to about 2-1/2" diameter and begin shaping the globe. (I prefer an oblong shape to a spherical globe.) Regardless of the shape you select, make sure that you leave about 1-1/2" of material at the top of the globe to allow you to hollow. If you remove too much material, you will get a lot of chatter when you attempt to hollow, and the piece may fly off the lathe.

After shaping the globe, mark the opening of the bottom of the tree topper. This will be the end toward the tailstock. Using a set of vernier calipers or a compass, mark about a 1" opening, then drill a 1/2" hole all the way through the globe. This hole will center the top and bottom of the globe.

Open the interior of the globe with a small squarenose scraper. This tool isn't a heavy tool, so when it starts to chatter, do not cut any deeper with it or you may have a nasty catch. Once you remove all the material you can with the squarenose scraper, switch to the small roundnose scraper and remove more material from the interior.

Be sure to use compressed air often to remove chips from the interior.

Now, switch to bent-angle tools to thin down the wall. To hollow something small, I rely on three bent-angle tools—a long, medium, and short—although you can generally get by with two, a long one and a short one. The short tool allows you to get around the initial opening, while the longer tools allow you to go deeper into the turning. The bent-angle tools I use are homemade. The shafts of the tools are 1/4" mild steel, and the tips are 3/16" high-speed steel. I weld the tips at about a 42-degree angle using Eutectic silver solder No. 1630XFC.

When hollowing the globe section of the tree topper, I actually alternate between using the bent-angle tools and the roundnose scraper. After using the bent-angle tools to get "around the corners" of the globe, I switch to a straight roundnose scraper.

The scraper is easier to control when hollowing the final one-third of the globe. Once I have the piece hollowed to about 1/8" thick, I refine the top, reducing the area that allowed me to hollow without a lot of chatter.

When you're pleased with the wall thickness, sand the piece and part it from the lathe.

At this point, the globe may be considered finished. As alternate designs, you can paint it, carve it, burn it, or dye it. Two variations are shown.

Turn the finial

Turn the finial from straight-grained stock about 1-3/8 × 8" long. Mount the piece in a chuck with spigot jaws. The spigot jaws extend out about 1-1/2", producing the solid grip required for turning without tailcenter support.

A bent-angle tool is essential in removing stock from inside the globe.

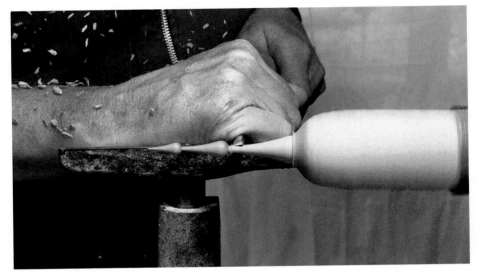

When turning the finial, always leave adequate mass at the base to dampen vibration. A small round skew and 1/2" roughing-out gouge are ideal for this task.

Switch to a small parting tool to turn the tenon that will fit into the globe.

With the finial stock held in the spigot jaws and the tail center in place, use the roughing-out gouge to turn a taper on what will become the top of the finial. Turn the roughing-out gouge on its side using the flat area of the tool.

Now, remove the tail center and use the skew to refine the top segment of the finial. I use the small spindle gouge to round over each segment on the finial. Sand each segment and apply sanding sealer before proceeding to the next one. The finial will be too delicate to sand after turning all the segments.

The first segment dictates the length and size of the rest of the segments. Once you establish the first segment, each successive segment needs to be a little bit larger and a little bit longer. Turn segments 2, 3, and 4 using a roughing-out gouge on its side, followed by the skew and finally the spindle gouge.

Once the four segments are complete, use a spindle gouge to turn a cove and decorative steps at the base of the finial. After sanding and finishing this section, cut a tenon to fit into the ½" hole in the top of the globe. Undercut the tenon so it fits on the globe with no gaps. Finally, part the finial from the lathe and glue the finial into the globe.

Turn the funnel

At this point, you should have a completed globe with an attached finial. Now you need some attractive way to have the tree topper sit on the top of the tree.

Hold the funnel stock (about 1-3/8 × 4") in the spigot jaws and turn it into a cylindrical shape. Estimate the finished length of your funnel, then cut a tenon that will fit into the bottom of the tree- topper globe.

Using a spindle gouge and skew, shape the funnel, then drill a 1/2" hole through the bottom of the

To speed up hollowing of the funnel, remove stock with a 1/2" drill bit.

With a spindle gouge, enlarge the opening of the funnel. When completed, the tree leader (top) will fit into this opening.

funnel. With a small spindle gouge, open the interior of the funnel. Sand the funnel, apply sanding sealer, part from the lathe, and glue in place.

Apply the finish

All that remains is to apply a finish. Spray the completed tree topper with satin lacquer, then carefully buff with 0000 steel wool before applying a second coat.

If you prefer an oil finish, carefully apply oil to the pieces separately prior to assembly.

Bob Rosand is a professional turner and educator living in Bloomsburg, PA. He has been a frequent contributor to the AW Journal.

Heavenly Angels

Nick Cook

While serving on the board of a community arts organization, I agreed to create a turned wooden angel for the benefit "Angel Show." Even though that was a dozen years ago, I find joy in turning this project. Hope you'll find as much pleasure turning these angels as I have.

Material and tools

For this project, I use 3" squares of ash or hard maple, commonly sold as baseball bat blanks, in 36"-lengths.

Of course you can use other material as well. Pine and poplar are both inexpensive and well-suited if you paint the finished product.

For tools, I recommend having these sharpened and ready: 1-1/4" spindle roughing gouge, 3/8" bedan tool, 3/8" spindle gouge, 3/8" or 1/4" deep-fluted bowl gouge.

The project also requires a scroll chuck.

Turn the angel's body

Cut the squares into lengths of 4", 6", 8", and 10" or select lengths to suit your own needs. Turn the blanks between centers with a 1-1/4" roughing gouge and form a tenon approximately 2" x 3/8" at one end to fit a scroll chuck *(Photo 1)*.

After mounting the blank in the scroll chuck, true up the opposite end and turn a cone to about 1-1/2" of the tenon. Next, hollow the blank to match the exterior shape, leaving the walls about 3/16" thick *(Photo 2)*.

Several tools are suitable for hollowing. When I start in the center and work toward the final wall thickness, I've had good luck with a 3/8" spindle gouge. This step removes most of the weight, which

allows the angel to be used as an ornament or tree topper.

For turning the top of the angel, leave a short spigot inside the cone to accept the expansion jaws of the scroll chuck.

Remove the blank from the chuck and remount at the opposite end. This will allow you to remove the tenon and shape the angel's

AW 19:4, p44

Rough out between centers with a 1-1/4" roughing gouge. With a 3/8" bedan tool, cut a 2" x 3/8" tenon (for fitting the blank into a scroll chuck) in one end.

Mount the body in a scroll chuck, using the tenon. Shape the body first, then hollow the interior with a 1/2" spindle gouge. Hollow the interior to reduce weight—just in case someone wants to use the angel as an ornament. To mount the body with a scroll chuck in the next step, turn a spigot on the inside of the body.

To turn the head, reverse the blank, then expand the scroll chuck into the spigot. This allows you to remove the tenon and shape the angel's head to about a 1" diameter (inset).

head (Photo 3). For this step, I prefer a 3/8" or 1/2" spindle gouge ground to a fingernail shape; the long fingernail grind lets me produce fine details. I turn the head to about 1" diameter.

Sand the angel by stepping through 150-grit, 180-grit, and finally 220-grit sandpaper.

Finish decisions depend on wood species and personal taste. For ash, I apply a white pickling stain followed by a coat of clear satin lacquer. Allow to dry.

An angel gets its wings

No angel can fly without wings. For turned wings, I cut 5/4" x 4" ash into rounds approximately 3-1/2" in diameter.

Draw a line through the center in line with the grain direction. Next, drill two holes in the wing disc. The first is 3/4" diameter and it is drilled 5/8" from the edge on the line through the center. The second hole is 1-1/8" diameter and is drilled 3/4" from the opposite edge of the disc, also on the centerline. Refer to the illustration opposite. To reduce tearout, use Forstner bits at a drill press (Photo 4). Then bandsaw the wing discs (Photo 5).

I use a screw chuck with a spacer to mount the disc on the lathe (Photo 6). With a 1/4" or 3/8" bowl gouge, turn the first side just as you would shape the bottom of a bowl or shallow plate. Leave a small flat surface at the center to remount the piece on a glue block.

With medium CA glue, attach the wing blank to a 2" x 1" waste block mounted in the scroll chuck. I use solid maple or poplar for my waste blocks.

After the CA sets, turn the back side of the wings into a dish-like shape, leaving the wall thickness just under 1/8" (Photo 7). Either a 3/8" or 1/4" deep-fluted bowl gouge is perfect for the task. To avoid the gouge catching in the wing holes, turn at a speed in the 1,800 range.

Use extra care sanding the holey wings, stepping through 150, 180 and 220 grits. After sanding is complete, apply finish to match the angel's body.

Before separating the dish from the waste block, turn a 1/4" x 1/4" tenon on the bottom side *(Photo 7 inset)*. The tenon will fit into a 1/4"-diameter hole drilled into the back of the angel body. For this drilling step, I prop the angel with a sand bag *(Photo 8)*.

Before attaching the wings, use a bandsaw, scrollsaw, or coping saw to cut a space in the top and bottom holes to give the appearance of wings *(Photo 9 and pattern)*.

Wing options

Another wing style involves shaping safety wire or brass wire into a figure eight. Once twisted together, you can push the center of the wire into a small hole in the back of the angel.

Need a third option? With metal sheers, cut wings from brass, aluminum or even pewter. Pewter— the softest and easiest to work—is the most expensive of the three.

Don't forget the halo

I have never actually had my own halo, so I really don't know how to describe it. There are two styles of angel halos shown in the opening photo. The angel in the background has a halo turned as part of the head. The foreground angel has a 3/4"-diameter turned ring added to the head.

You also can bend a halo from safety wire or brass wire.

Nick Cook is a professional turner, teacher and writer living in Marietta, Georgia.

4 Before cutting circles for angel wings, mark a centerline on a 5/4" x 4" wide maple or ash stock. Draw a 3-1/2" circle and mark center for the 3/4" and 1-1/8" holes. Then bore the holes with a Forstner bit as shown.

5 After boring the holes, bandsaw the 3-1/2"-diameter wing discs.

6 To turn the outside of the angel wings, use two 1/4" plywood spacers to reduce the length of the screw penetration into the 5/4" stock.

7 Use a 3/8" bowl gouge to turn the interior of the bowl-shaped wings.

When finished, turn a 1/4" tenon (inset) on the back side of the wings. The wings attach to the body with the tenon.

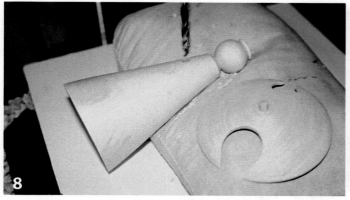

8

Prop and support the angel on a sandbag, then drill a 1/4" hole in the back of the body to fit the wing tenon. Use your hand to prevent the angel from rolling during the drilling procedure.

9

Using the pattern above as reference, cut the final wing shape with a bandsaw, scrollsaw or coping saw.

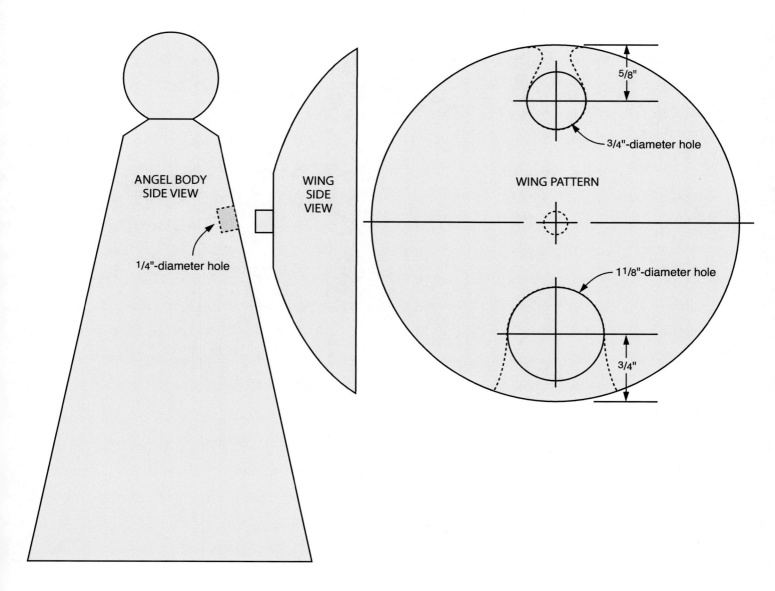

ANGEL BODY
SIDE VIEW

1/4"-diameter hole

WING
SIDE
VIEW

WING PATTERN

5/8"

3/4"-diameter hole

1 1/8"-diameter hole

3/4"

Burl Turned into Angels

Linda Van Gehuchten

Photo: John Hetherington

I f you can turn a bowl, complete a basic spindle-turning project, and feel comfortable with a bit of carving, you can complete this heavenly project for holiday gift-giving.

Get started
For lathe tools, you'll need a small bowl gouge (I prefer a 3/8" gouge), 1/2" spindle gouge, 1/2" skew, spindle roughing gouge,

texturing tool, and parting tool. You'll also need a 4-jaw scroll chuck or faceplate.

For turning stock, cut the angel's body from a 3 × 3 × 2" piece of figured burl. (Burl lends itself well to this project, but other natural-edge pieces would also work.) Mount the burl on a 2 × 2 × 1-1/2" wasteblock.

For the angel's head and halo, use a piece of 2×2×4" hard maple.

The remainder of this maple piece will be used for the base.

The project also requires a 3–4" piece of 3/32" brass welding rod, a 3-1/2 × 1/2" scrap of raw leather, and a short piece of 3/16" dowel.

Prepare the wood
Mount the wasteblock in your faceplate or 4-jaw scroll chuck. True up the wasteblock so its face is flat.

AW 21:3, p26

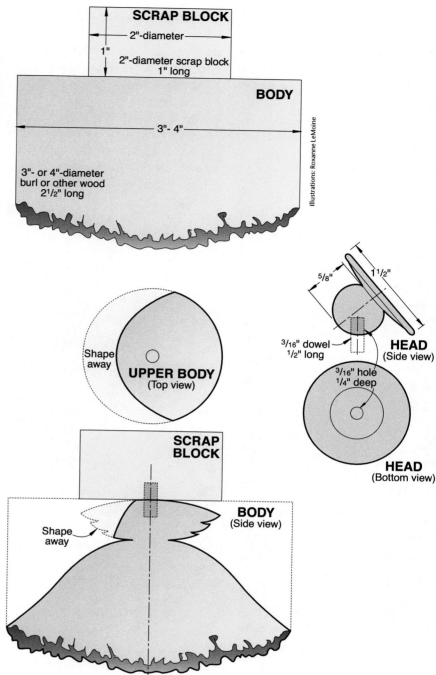

Illustrations: Roxanne LeMoine

Drill a 3/16" hole into the face of the wasteblock. Glue a length of 3/16" dowel into the drilled hole; trim the dowel so it sticks out 3/8".

You will use this 3/16" dowel hole as the top of the angel to join the head to the body and to help you reverse-chuck the angel.

Flatten the top of the burl (this will be the top of the angel) where it will meet the wasteblock. On this surface, find its center and drill a 3/16" hole 3/8" deep. Dry-fit the burl blank into the wasteblock with the dowel. If the burl sits flat, you are ready to glue together the wasteblock and burl.

Spread cyanoacrylate (CA) glue on the burl side and spray the catalyst on the wasteblock; join the two pieces and give them a little twist to hold till the glue sets (about 10 seconds). The dowel helps align the wasteblock and the burled skirt for the glue up.

The wasteblock will allow you to shape the torso by giving you more room for your turning tools. Now, bring up the tailstock on the lathe bed for support (Photo 1).

With an uneven surface on the burl, the live center is not always engaged properly. To solve this problem, flatten away the center of the burl with a small power carver—just enough for the live center to sit properly. Take care not to damage the outer natural edge.

Turn the skirt exterior

With the 3/8" bowl gouge, turn the outside of the bowl until you eliminate flat spots on the natural edge. You want to keep a clean outside edge on the bark, so begin the cuts from the outside of the rim.

Since this is a natural-edge project with little sharp spikes that want to grab the gouge, begin the cut with the flute of the gouge facing the direction of the cut. This prevents the edges and spikes of the burl grabbing the tool.

Shape the outside of the bowl, leaving about 5/8" for the angel's torso.

Turn the skirt interior

Look at the profile above; the smallest diameter would be close to where the waist will be.

Just a reminder: Have the center (tip) of the bowl gouge cutting at center or just above to achieve a clean cut.

Next, sand and finish the interior of the bowl. (I prefer a shellac friction polish such as Shellawax EEE.)

For the last detail, make a small mark for the center. This is your reference mark for a 3/32" brass welding rod that will support the angel on its stand.

Turn the torso
Work back and forth between the outside skirt profile and the torso until you are satisfied with the shape of both (Photo 2).

Power-sand the natural edge with a disc sander with 180 and 220 grits on a power drill. Hand-sand through 320, 500, 1000, 2000, 4000 grits. Then apply a friction polish and wax. Buff with a paper towel. Don't use a cotton rag or cloth, which could wrap around a finger and draw your hand into the rotating piece.

For a clean cut in tight areas like the waist, use a skew with the long point down. Sand and finish the remainder of the exterior.

On the underside of the torso, make two or three shallow grooves with the skew point (Photo 3). In another step, you'll use these as wing references.

Reverse-chuck the torso
To shape the top of the turning, cut away at the wasteblock to give you more room (Photo 4). Before parting off the angel body, sand and finish.

Reverse-chuck the angel to finish off the torso, using a buffing ball and the tailstock to hold the angel securely (Photo 5).

Shape the turned torso
Take a close look at the skirt, and select the best grain for the front of the angel. From the top, make a mark down the center with a pencil. Now, draw a curve using the centerline as a reference (Photo 6). This will be your guide to shape the torso. Shape the torso with a homemade sanding disc that fits in your 4-jaw chuck (Photo 7).

Hold a hand-carving tool short in one hand and the angel body in the other. Using the lines under the torso as a starting point, lay one cutting edge of the gouge in a turned

groove, and roll and cut a curve on the face of the torso. (A skew creates the same effect.) This cut implies the feathers and wings.

Turn the head and halo
With a spindle roughing gouge, turn the 2×2×4" maple piece between centers. Then use a parting tool to turn a spigot so you can hold it in your chuck.

Mount the stock in the 4-jaw chuck. With a spindle gouge, turn the profile of the head and halo. Refer to the drawings. Hold the head and halo against the body to see if the head is sized proportionally.

With the skew, make a small indentation for the angel's mouth, which will be right on center. The skew is also the perfect tool for cleaning up the front face of the halo where it meets the head. You may add some lines near the rim to highlight the halo. Sand and finish the head and front of the halo. Part off the halo and head section (*Photo 8*). Then reverse-chuck and finish the back of the halo.

Texture the halo top

Switch the standard jaws on the chuck for the step jaws or small jaws. Using a 3-1/2 × 1/2" strip of raw leather, wrap the head of the angel (to avoid denting) and clamp the head in the chuck jaws (*Photo 9*).

Use a small bowl gouge to shape and clean up the halo top. Sand and finish the top of the halo.

For the swirling pattern on the back of the halo, use a texturing tool (*Photo 10*). Keep the tool rest about 3" from the halo, tilt the tool to 45 degrees, get the tool spinning by touching the wood with a little pressure, run it back and forth once, and the swirl is done.

Assemble the angel

The point on the head for the drill-bit entry requires two intersecting lines. First, draw a line from the mouth down to the chin. Then

hold the angel and the head in the position where it will go on the body. Use the first line drawn to center the head on the body, then draw a line on the side of the head to indicate the angle for the dowel to join the parts. Extend these lines until they intersect. Refer to the drawings.

With an awl, make an indentation. Using a 3/16" brad-point bit held in a drill press, drill the hole in the head, relying on the indentation as the starting point and the pencil line on the side of the head as a guide for the angle. Drill the hole about 1/4" deep.

Glue a 3/16" dowel onto the head. Then cut the dowel so it sticks out of the head about 1/4".

On the body, drill out the piece of dowel left in the top. Dry-fit the head on the body. Shorten the dowel if needed so that the head rests on the body.

If the back of the wing/torso is in the way of the halo, carve out a niche for the halo. Glue the head to the body.

Turn the stand

Turn the stand from the leftover maple. Drill a 3/32"-diameter hole for the brass welding rod. Cut the rod to 3".

Push the rod into the stand. Drill a 3/32" hole into the underside of the body to accept the rod (*Photo 11*).

Linda Van Gehuchten is a former AAW board member. She lives in Sarver, Pennsylvania, and is a long-time member of Turners Anonymous in the Pittsburgh area.

Angel Ornament

This design also makes a popular ornament. For this, drill a 1/8" hole into the halo and just under the head. (This hides the ribbon knot for the hanger.)

Use an 8" length of 1/8"-wide ribbon for the loop. Thread both ends through the hole, make a knot, and pull the ribbon tight so the loop is on the back-side of the halo.

11

Tree-Trimming Medallion

Bob Rosand

If you turn and market Christmas ornaments, you'll find that every year you need to come up with a new ornament, or at least a new variation on the ornaments that you already have.

This point was succinctly made one year when a good customer came into my booth looking for something "different." When I didn't have a "new and improved" Christmas ornament, she responded by saying, "Oh," and exited the booth without buying anything.

The medallion came about because I was trying to come up with a new ornament, and also trying to provide a canvas on wood for my wife, Susan. I also had a lot of scraps and cutoffs that were just too good to throw away, but not big enough for bowls or platters.

When I started writing this article, I was a bit concerned that people would not attempt turning this ornament because they could not paint. Fortunately, that is not a problem. If you can paint or have a spouse who paints, this project is great. But you can make numerous variations without being skilled in art. The first is not to paint the ornament at all, but simply to turn the ornament and accentuate the wood. You also can texture the center of the medallion with a Sorby texturing tool or a chatterwork tool.

A second method is to make stencils or purchase them at a crafts supply store and stencil a decoration such as a wreath, reindeer, Christmas tree, dove, or snowflake in the center of the ornament.

A third method is to purchase appropriate ink stamps, stamp the center of the ornament, and then use a pyrography tool to burn the stamp into the ornament. If your penmanship is good, consider customizing the ornament with the year or with the name of a grandchild. Be creative and come up with your own variations.

Get started

For turning tools you will need a 1/2" or 3/4" spindle roughing gouge, 3/8" spindle gouge, parting tool, 1/2" beading tool (I use an Ashley Iles tool), and texturing tool (I use the Sorby model).

For turning stock, use end-grain scraps about 4-1/2 × 4-1/2 × 1/2". End grain works great, especially with the texturing tool or the chatterwork tool, but side grain also works.

The pieces shown on these pages are turned from ambrosia maple.

Turn the front

Sand one face of the blank flat on a belt sander and glue it, centered, to a wasteblock. For end grain, use a 3/4" spindle roughing gouge to true up the outside of the blank. For side grain, use a standard spindle gouge. Turn the blank to a 4" diameter. Then use a spindle gouge to true up the face of the blank. Note that the tool is turned on its side with the flute pointed in the direction of travel (toward the center). The bevel is rubbing, giving control of the tool. Do not cut with the tip of the tool.

Next define the perimeter of the ornament with three beads with the flute pointed down (*Photo 1*). With the rim complete, use the spindle gouge to slightly hollow the center of the medallion.

If it helps, think of the medallion as a small plate, which it essentially is. If you plan to use a stamp or stencil on the center section, make the medallion a bit flatter so you don't have trouble

AW 23:3, p30

transferring the stencil or making an impression with the stamp. Now use the spindle gouge to round over the edge of the medallion and start shaping the back. Finish-sand the face of the ornament and the turned portion of the back.

Detail the back

For me, now comes the fun part. To finish the back of the ornament, reverse the disc and hold it in a vacuum chuck.

If you don't have a vacuum chuck, make a jam chuck from a wasteblock and friction-fit the medallion into it. When making multiple medallions, carefully turn each medallion to fit one jam chuck, or make a new jam chuck for each different-size medallion.

I always had a difficult time centering work on the vacuum chuck; it was always off just a bit. The solution is incredibly simple.

First measure the inside diameter of the tailstock quill with calipers. Measuring with the calipers, turn a taper on the wasteblock of the medallion *(Photo 2)*, part it off, reverse it, and place the taper into the tailstock quill. Slide the tailstock up to the headstock, press the medallion against the vacuum chuck *(Photo 3)*, and turn on the vacuum pump. The piece should be perfectly centered. Just to be safe, put the tail center in place to hold the medallion while turning the back.

When most of the back is turned, back off the tailstock and turn away the remains of the wasteblock *(Photo 4)*. Take gentle cuts or you may pop the piece loose.

With the back of the medallion turned and sanded, you can texture or finish it. I used a Sorby texturing tool to cut decorative spiral lines *(Photos 5 and 6)*.

Use the tool as a scraper with the cutting end of the tool angled

1 Use a beading tool to cut three beads into the rim of the medallion.

3 Insert the medallion taper into the tailstock quill and press it against the vacuum chuck.

5 Texture the back of the ornament with a Sorby texturing tool.

2 Turn a tapered tenon on the medallion wasteblock using calipers to check the diameter.

4 Back off the tailstock and carefully turn away the remaining small tenon.

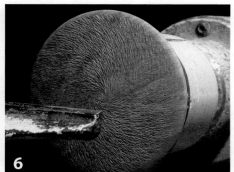

6 The Sorby texturing tool cuts a beautiful spiral pattern.

down and the handle up. I also tilt the head of the tool to about a 45-degree angle. Engage the tool at the edge of the medallion and move it toward the center. It is important to get the cutterhead rotating before moving the tool along the tool rest. If you don't, you risk getting scratch marks as the tool begins to rotate. Experiment with different cutterhead orientations to make different texture patterns.

Now decorate the medallion. Don't forget to drill a 1/16"-diameter hole at the top of the medallion for hanging on a Christmas tree.

Finally, apply a finish (I use Deft satin lacquer).

Bob Rosand is a professional turner and educator living in Bloomsburg, PA. He has been a frequent contributor to the AW *Journal.*

Ornamental Snowflakes

Jon Magill

Ornamental turning, or OT, rarely appears in the same sentence with "production work." Yet here is a production technique that will allow you to create multiple ornaments relatively quickly and easily.

The foundation of this particular technique rests with the jig (really just a socket) into which you place a blank for cutting on one side. It's easy to reverse the blank and then cut a pattern on the other side. The result is a simple-to-make, two-sided ornament. Or in this case, you can turn a collection of thin snowflakes.

Make a socket

Begin by making the socket itself out of a piece of 1/4"-thick hardwood. Rough-cut the wood into a disc appropriate to grip in your chuck. Drill a hole in the center of your disc to allow mounting onto a wasteblock with a central screw and a fender washer (or use your tailstock). Once mounted, true the outer edge to a diameter that will work with your chuck jaws. Cut a tenon about half the thickness of the disc to grip with the jaws. Leave a shoulder to register against the face of the jaws.

Transfer the disc to your chuck with tower jaws and cut or drill through the center to open up the middle of the disc.

Move the chuck and jig to the rose-engine lathe. Before you start cutting, a few simple steps will help avoid some of the obscure pitfalls that could prevent your jig and blanks from mating.

First, ensure that your headstock is oscillating about a vertically

With the help of a jig, you can create a blizzard of creative ornaments.

centered position (swinging the same distance toward you and away from you as it rotates). Second, check that your cutting frame is set exactly at the correct center height. If either of these is not done, there will be distortions in your pattern—both the hole in the socket and the outside of the blanks. These distortions may prevent your jig from holding the blanks.

Finally, make sure that your slide rest is perfectly parallel with your lathe's headstock. You can do this by holding a straightedge against the headstock and along the edge of the long portion of your slide rest. This adjustment will keep your jig and blanks from being cut at a tapered angle.

Using a horizontal cutting frame, or HCF, open up the socket

in the disc to a size appropriate for your final ornaments. The tower jaws allow the head of the cutting frame to pass completely through the disc, creating parallel sides without hitting the inside of the chuck. If you do not have tower jaws, you will need to devise an alternate technique.

The final size of the cut-through opening should be slightly smaller than the stock size you plan to use for your ornaments. Stock in the 2"- to 3"-diameter range seems to work well for this project.

Mark your disc at each edge of the #1 jaw on your chuck. Remove the jig and sand if necessary to clean up the front and back faces of the disc. Then make two small blocks to span the opening, leaving a space through the center, and glue these to the inside of the disc. (Hot-melt adhesive

AW 23:4, p34

Using wasteblock and 4-jaw chuck secured to a wood lathe, cut a tenon and leave a shoulder on the 1/4" disc for the jig.

Using a horizontal cutting frame and holding the disc in tower jaws, cut the socket all the way through the disc to make the jig.

Cut along the outside of the cylinder to create the end-grain blanks that will be sliced off. Check the fit by sliding the jig onto the cylinder.

Two jig discs and several blanks are ready for rose-engine detailing. Blocks glued to the back of the lower jig provide backing and allow reversing the blanks.

Mark the jig on the inside, indicating the left and right edges of the #1 jaw of the chuck. The shoulder and tenon on the disc work as normal.

Make a series of cuts, adding phasing for interest, across the first face. Reverse the blank and cut the other face to finish the ornamental snowflake.

is perfect for this application.) Make sure the blocks are small enough to clear the inside edges of your chuck jaws. These blocks provide backing for the blanks when they are placed into the socket of the jig.

Prepare your blanks

Prepare some blanks using spindle-oriented stock. The goal is to end up with slices of end-grain material for your blanks. True up cylinders to slightly larger than the outside diameter (OD) required, with a tenon on one end. Good choices if you are making snowflake designs include white woods like holly and hornbeam, or alternative materials like faux ivory. Any wood that can be painted is fine too. Acrylic interference medium paints in reds and greens, over a coat of white, add a nice holiday sparkle.

With a cylinder mounted in your chuck (*Photo 1*), mark off thicknesses (1/4", or the same thickness as your disc) and use a thin parting tool to cut grooves slightly deeper than the "peaks" will be (otherwise the peaks may be damaged when separating each blank off the main cylinder). Move the cylinder to the rose-engine lathe and cut the outside profile by slowly feeding into, and then along the length of, the cylinder (*Photo 2*). Keep your jig handy to check for fit as you work down to the final diameter. Remove the stock and slice off the individual blanks using a bandsaw, handsaw, or parting tool (*Photo 3*).

Turn a snowflake

Using a couple dabs of hot-melt adhesive, mount a blank into the socket (*Photo 4*). Mount the chuck that holds the jig onto the rose-engine lathe. Place the disc into the chuck and align your #1 jaw marks (*Photo 5*). Make a light cut around the periphery of the blank, then stop the lathe and cutting frame, and check that the "points" of the snowflake are aligned with the jig's points (*Photo

6*). If adjustment is necessary, open the chuck slightly to rotate the disc as needed, then retighten.

Proceed through a sequence of cuts on one face, remove the jig, and use your thumbs through the back of the disc to pop out the blank. Reverse the blank into the jig with another couple drops of hot-melt glue and cut the second face.

For the truly adventurous, piercing all the way through the center portion of your ornaments creates an even more delicate version of these snowflakes.

Drill carefully to add hangers or thread to display your new batch of snowflakes on the tree.

Jon Magill is an ornamental turner who lives in Clinton, WA. He is a member of the Seattle chapter of the AAW and Ornamental Turners International, an AAW chapter dedicated to ornamental turning

Colorful Christmas Lights

Judy Chestnut

This past Christmas, I gave more than 60 Christmas bulbs as gifts—and not one required an electrical outlet.

You can turn these light bulbs in a variety of sizes for different uses. I have made them for Christmas tree ornaments, decorations for holiday wraps, and turned smaller versions for necklaces and earrings.

For this project, my favorite wood is Dymondwood. Although the laminations are slightly more difficult to turn, it does make an attractive bulb like the examples shown here.

Once you get started, it is easy to turn these in multiple quantities because it doesn't take much more time to make six than it does to make one.

I've collected Christmas ornaments since 1970. This design was partially inspired by an ornament Chip Siskey brought to one of our Kansas City-area AAW chapter holiday parties.

Select stock and tools

I recommend the first time you make these, choose a wood that is easy to turn. Padauk (for the bulb) and yellowheart (for the threads) work well. You'll also need a 1/4" birch dowel.

I suggest you use whatever tools you are most comfortable with and happen to own. I turn my Christmas bulbs with micro (also called mini or detail) tools. If you turn these bulbs with larger tools, use a light touch.

Cut the blanks

The padauk blank is 1" square and 1-3/4" long. The yellowheart is 3/4" square by 5/8" long. For this part, I slice pen blanks up in 5/8" lengths. Cut the 1/4" birch dowel 2-1/4" long.

I mount my stock in a Beall collet chuck with a 1/4" collet. If you do not have a collet chuck, a set of spigot jaws will work. Just cut the yellowheart blank long enough to mount in the chuck and eliminate the 1/4" dowel.

For me, the dowel serves a dual purpose. The dowel makes it quick and easy to mount and turn multiple bulbs. In addition, I leave enough dowel on the bulb to serve as the filament contact portion when I part off the bulb from the headstock.

Photos: Judy Chesnut and Vickie McCla

Drill the blanks and glue the parts

Mark the centers on the yellow-heart and padauk. I drill with a size F bit so that the hole is slightly larger than 1/4". This produces a snug fit, but not so tight that it splits the blanks. If you don't have a size F drill bit, you can lightly sand the dowel so it doesn't fit in the hole too tightly.

Using a vise or clamp to hold the stock, drill a hole 5/8" deep in the end of the padauk. Drill completely through the yellow-heart as shown in *Photo A*.

Assemble the three pieces with cyanoacrylate (CA) glue.

Mount the bulb stock

Mount the blank on the lathe as shown in *Photo B*. I like to leave just enough dowel exposed to safely part it off with a small skew when finished. This reduces the chance of vibration or of the dowel breaking.

Snug the tailstock, then begin turning

It is important to bring up the tailstock and check it often to be sure it remains snug. If you try to turn this without the tailstock, the dowel will twist and break.

Using a light touch, turn the bulb to a cylinder. Check your tailstock again and be sure it is snug, but not too tight. Begin shaping the bulb with a 3/8" spindle gouge, taking light cuts.

Turn the bulb shape

For reference while turning, it is helpful to have a real Christmas bulb in front of you. At this point, I suggest holding a dark-colored bulb up to the stock and lightly touch the bulb to the padauk while the lathe is turning. This leaves a line around the wood, which marks the widest part of the bulb as shown in *Photo C*. I cut downhill from that line, which simplifies shaping.

Beads sub for threads

Instead of threads, I turn three beads on the yellowheart. This gives the appearance of threads and they are much easier to turn.

Refine the shape

After cutting the beads, refine the shape of the bulb. leaving just enough at the tailstock end to keep the bulb stable. I do most of my sanding at this point, beginning at 220 grit and working through 600 grit.

With a small skew or gouge, gently part off the bulb at the tailstock end as shown in *Photo D*. Finish-sand as necessary.

Apply finish

Apply the finish while the bulb is still mounted in the chuck. I've had good luck applying a sanding sealer and then friction polish. With the lathe running at a slow speed (500 rpm), buff with a soft paper towel.

Don't use too much muscle on this step as the dowel can easily twist off.

With a marker, add detail

Stop the lathe and add a black line around the dowel next to the beads as shown in *Photo E*. Rotate the lathe by hand and support the marker on the tool rest. I prefer a flat-tip calligraphy pen, because it makes a neater line than a round tip. These pens are available at office-supply or art stores.

Parting off from lathe

With a small skew, part off the dowel at the edge of the black line, leaving about 1/8" of dowel on the bulb as shown in *Photo F*.

Final touches

Using a #60 drill bit, drill a small hole in the center of the dowel about 1/2" deep as shown in *Photo G*. I have not found a screweye small enough for this ornament, so I use the eye from a #202 brass fishing hook.

Before gluing the shank into the bulb, paint the end of the dowel with a silver Sharpie pen (available at office-supply stores) as shown in *Photo H*.

Finally, adhere the shank of the fishing hook into the bulb with CA glue as shown in *Photo I*.

AAW member Judy Chestnut (twoskibums@ earthlink.net) is vice president of the Kansas City Woodturners Club.

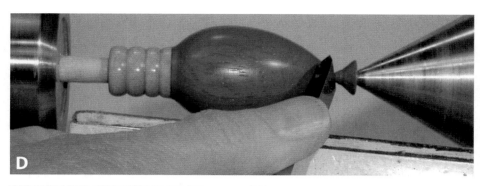

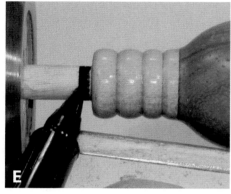

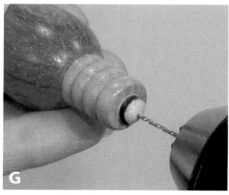

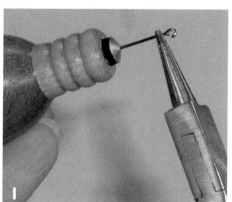

Santa Claus Nutcracker

Bonnie Klein

Making a turned nutcracker has been high on my list of things to do for a long time. When the classes at the local Woodcraft Store for last fall were being lined up, I committed to doing one on turning a Santa nutcracker. That meant I needed to get cracking!

I gathered all the pictures, books, and anything I could put my hands on that had anything to do with nutcrackers. I visited the year-round holiday shops and studied the nutcrackers. I soon realized how expensive and how poorly made most of them were. It was a good challenge!

I had several requirements: I wanted my nutcracker to be as large as possible and still be turned on a small lathe. The size was not much of a problem, because the body section and legs would be separate turnings. For the class, we turned the body, head, and hat as one piece, but these could be turned separately for different styles or a taller nutcracker.

My nutcracker needed a crank, but I didn't want to have to chisel out for the crank. Instead, I laminated the body together in thirds, with the center section in two pieces, leaving a gap of the desired size and shape.

I wanted all the parts to be easy to put together, so I decided to use one axis for both the jaw crank and the arm joint. This made assembly easier and disassembly possible for painting and decorating. I turned each arm and mitten as a single turning, cut it at the elbow, beveled it, and glued it back together. I also turned each leg and boot as a single turning, cut the toe, beveled it,

and glued it back together to shape the boot.

Eight students were in the class, most had minimal or no turning experience, and they all finished all the turnings for the Santa in the one-day class. It was a good test of the project design. They did the painting at home, I hope.

I am pleased to share this idea with you and hope it inspires you to make some for the holiday season. Make a full-sized working drawing and from that make a template or story stick for each part.

Body

I was able to find pine stair tread material that was 1-1/8 inch thick to laminate together for the body. The prototype in the photo has a

narrow crank area—not good for nuts. The drawing provides a wider crank area—much better! Make sure

The Santa Claus nutcracker is constructed of simple turnings: as with the holidays, the spirit is reflected in the decoration. The body of Mrs. Claus, left, is turned and awaiting paint. Laminating the blank eliminates the need to chisel out the crank area.

Photo: Rick Mastelli

AW 124, p13

The body is laminated to include the gap for the crank, then turned before the crank is installed. One end of the crank serves as the cracker jaw, the other is a handle at Santa's back, which you squeeze to crack the nut.

the grain of the crank is running lengthwise for strength. While the body section was still square, I found it to be a convenient time to drill 1/4-inch holes for the leg tenons and a 1/4-inch hole through the body for the arm and crank axis.

The first thing you will need to decide is where the mouth is to open. On most traditional nutcrackers I looked at, the mouth opening was right at the neck line. I preferred to have the mouth opening a little above the neck in order to have lips and a place for the beard. Don't make the neck line too low because you need to have enough room for a shoulder above the arm axis.

Mount between centers, turn the body section round, use your template to mark off the hat, neck, belt and fur hem locations, and turn these shapes. Turn the bottom of the body flat, so the legs will join well. For unrestricted arm movements, the shoulders should be wider than the rest of the body. After turning the body shape, fit the cracker crank to open and close all the way, and trim it to match the contour of the face profile. A short section of 1/4-inch dowel holds the crank in place, leaving space for the arm tenons.

Arms

Turn the arms between centers from 1 inch diameter pieces. Using your template, mark out the locations of the cuff and mitten and turn the desired shape. Cut the arm at the elbow and bevel the cut on a belt or disc sander to create the desired bend to the arm. Glue the arm back together and do the necessary sanding to smooth the joint. Carve the mittens to create a thumb or desired hand shape. I drilled the arm pieces after they were finished in order to better position them, using a 1/4-inch drill bit and gluing in a short section of 1/4-inch dowel. These arms are not glued to the body, but rather are a friction fit in order to position them as desired or to remove them for disassembling the nutcracker.

Legs

Turn the legs between centers from 1-1/2 inch diameter stock. Using your template, mark out the locations of the boot cuff and turn the desired shape. I think the boots need to look like they have a cuff turned over at the top with the pants tucked into the boots. Leave a tenon about 1/4 inch long and 1/4 inch

in diameter at the top of the leg to position the leg on the body. Cut the turning as the drawing shows, using about two-thirds of the scrap to create the boot toe by beveling, sanding, gluing, and refining. Make sure the Santa will stand upright before gluing the legs to the body.

Pockets, nose, and belt buckle

The pockets are made from one turning shaped like a tiny bowl, then cut in half and sanded to fit the contour of the coat. The nose is a bell-shaped turning, cut and sanded to fit the contour of the face. The belt buckle is shaped from a small rectangular scrap of wood. Glue these to the body.

Painting and decorating

I used acrylic paint from the local art store for most of the Santa. I found a thicker paint used for decorating fabric, that worked very well for the textured look of the fur ruff on the coat hem, sleeves, hat hem, and tassel. The paint comes in a small bottle with a tiny nozzle that is designed for making dots or lines on fabric. I simply made dots close together creating the texture I was looking for. The beard, mustache, eyebrows, and hair are made from fur fabric found in a fabric store and glued onto the head with tacky glue. For the beard, I glued a strip on the crank at the top edge, but also glued some on both sides of the chest to create a wider, more Santa-like beard.

I plan to make small toys to fill the pockets and put some tree decorations in his hands. Mrs. Claus has been turned and is awaiting paint. The possibilities are endless!

Bonnie Klein, Kenton, WA, is a professional turner and popular demonstrator.

Holiday Nutcracker

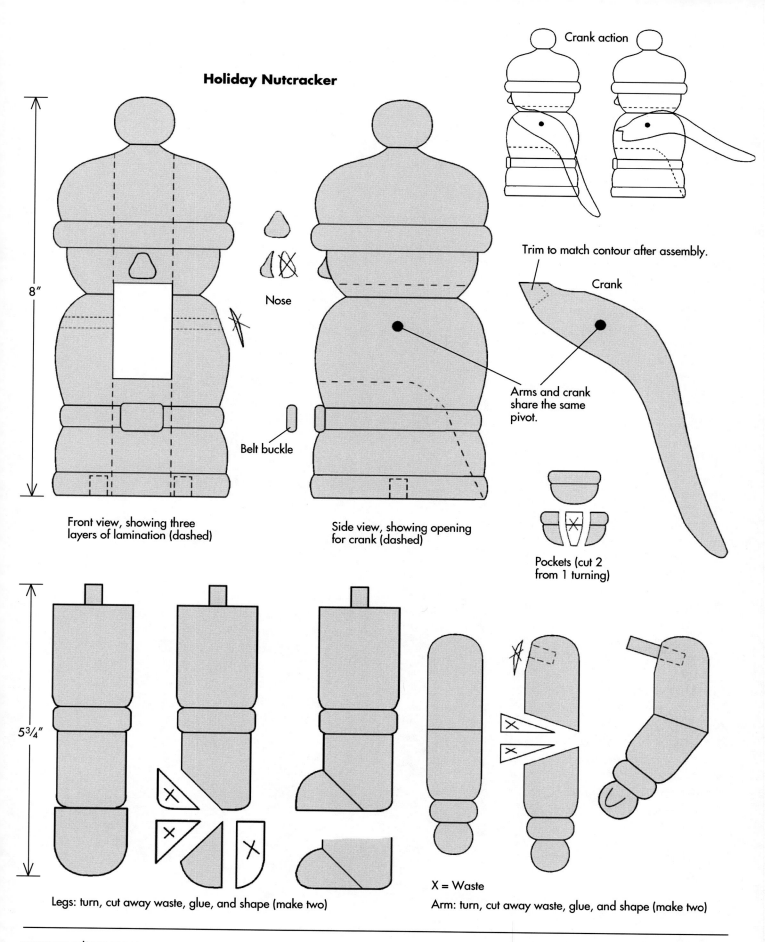

Crank action

Nose

Belt buckle

Trim to match contour after assembly.

Crank

Arms and crank share the same pivot.

Pockets (cut 2 from 1 turning)

8"

Front view, showing three layers of lamination (dashed)

Side view, showing opening for crank (dashed)

5³/₄"

Legs: turn, cut away waste, glue, and shape (make two)

X = Waste

Arm: turn, cut away waste, glue, and shape (make two)

Tiny Acorn Ornaments

Bob Rosand

I've made a career out of turning Christmas tree ornaments. I've probably turned close to 6,000 ornaments—the ones with a hollow globe and the four-segmented icicle—over the last 10 to 15 years. I've also turned a couple thousand of my "regular" birdhouse ornaments—the ones with multiple parts. These are all good sellers, but if you do crafts shows, you need a good price range of items as customers will part with a $20 bill much faster than a fifty or a Ben Franklin.

The birdhouse ornaments and my standard ornaments represent the higher end of my ornaments, so I realized I needed something to fill in that $20 to $25 gap. What I came up with is an acorn birdhouse ornament. It is far less complicated than my "regular" birdhouse ornament, has fewer parts, is easier to make, and sells well.

Getting started

Most turners have the required lathe tools for the acorn ornament. You'll need a small skew, a spindle gouge, a round-nosed scraper, a small square- nosed scraper, and a spindle roughing gouge. The body of the acorn is made with square straight-grained stock about 4" long and 1-1/4" square. Walnut, oak, maple, and cherry are all good choices for the acorn body.

AW 18:3, p44

While the stock is square, I drill a 1/4" hole about 1/2" deep for the entry to the birdhouse and a 1/16" or smaller hole below that for the birdhouse perch. I place the 1/4" entry hole lower than I want it on the finished product. This allows me to reverse chuck, glue the piece in place, and part it off where I think the entry hole should be.

Although you can certainly use contrasting domestic woods, I turn the cap from scrap burl pieces about 2" square and 1-1/2" high. I make the perch from odds and ends of ebony.

Turn the acorn body

The easiest method I have found for turning the body is to chuck it in a Talon chuck with spigot jaws. I like the Talon because of its small size and the spigot jaws hold extremely well. If you don't have a Talon chuck, or don't want to spend the money on one, no problem. Fasten a waste block to a small faceplate, then true the waste block and drill a 1" hole about 1" deep. Turn a 1" tenon on the body of the acorn body stock and glue it into the waste block. It's a little more time-consuming, but just as effective.

Place the stock for the body of the acorn in the chuck and use a roughing-out gouge to turn it to a cylinder. Then smooth that cylinder with a small skew (Photo A). Stop the lathe and make a pencil line at the hole where the perch will be. I don't turn away any more wood from this point. Here's why: When I turn the perch and glue it in place later, I want it to stick straight out and not angle up or down. This is not an issue with the 1/4" entry hole since nothing is being glued into it. Although a small detail, this will either make or break the look of the ornament.

I begin shaping the acorn body with a 3/8" spindle gouge. From the perch pencil line, taper towards the top slightly. Then begin to turn what will be the bottom of the acorn body. Be careful not to remove too much material from this base, because you will need to hollow the interior. Once you have the shape where you want it, use a 3/8" or 1/2" drill to open the interior (Photo B) followed by a round-nosed scraper.

I don't worry about extreme thinness here; I just want to lessen the weight of the ornament so that

it doesn't weigh down the branch of a tree.

Once the hollowing is complete, I return to the bottom of the acorn and continue refining that, before parting it from the lathe. You will probably notice that no sanding has taken place prior to parting the acorn body from the lathe. That is because you'll reverse the turning and friction-fit it to the waste material already in the chuck (Photo C).

Using a small skew laid flat, peel down, making a tenon that the acorn body fits on to. The fit only needs to be snug, because you'll adhere it with super glue. Now, complete your final shaping, sanding, and parting from the lathe (Photo D).

Cap on the house

As mentioned earlier, I turn my acorn caps from scrap pieces of burl about 2" in diameter and about 1-1/2" in length. I then glue the burl scrap to a waste block held in my chuck. The waste blocks are always pieces of oak, maple, or cherry. I never use plywood, even though it may be tempting, as the plys are notorious for separating

Turn the body of the acorn birdhouse, leaving sufficient material at the base for hollowing. Note the pencil line at the opening for the perch; it should be untouched.

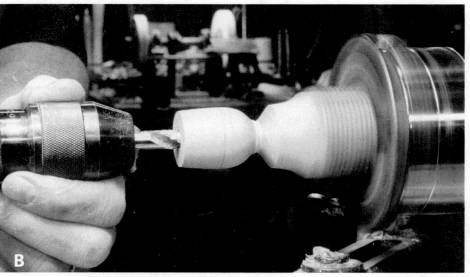

Use a 3/8" drill bit to drill out the interior of the acorn birdhouse.

while you are turning, resulting in a destroyed piece.

Next, fit the acorn body to the cap *(Photo E)*. True up the sides and the face of the burl cap in the lathe. The stock closest to the tailstock will be the underside of the cap. Undercut this a bit—just for aesthetics—and then use a set of vernier calipers to mark the diameter of the top of the acorn body. Using a spindle gouge, remove some of the interior of the cap to reduce the weight. Then cut a rabbet for the body to fit into with a square-nosed scraper.

Once the pieces fit properly *(Photo F)*, I refine the shape of the acorn cap *(Photos G and H)*, part it from the lathe, reverse it, and friction-fit it to a waste block *(Photo I)*. This friction-fitting allows you to refine the shape a bit more, sand it, and drill a hole for a screw-eye hole for hanging.

Once complete, you can glue the cap to the body of the acorn birdhouse. If you get a little tired of sanding, you might consider using a Sorby texturing tool to texture the roof of your birdhouse *(Photo J)*. I have done this with great success. It is no replacement for clean cutting and a sharp tool, but if you do it properly, you don't have to pick up a piece of sandpaper.

The perch

All that remains is to turn the perch. Ebony is a perfect species. With the perch held in the chuck, use a small round skew to "peel" down to about a 1/16" diameter *(Photos K and L)*. I also turn a small spherical shape at the base of the perch. This is more for aesthetics than anything, but the little globe section also keeps the perch from going too far into the body of the acorn as well as giving me a bit more of a glue area. Using a small parting tool and a set of vernier calipers, turn a tenon to

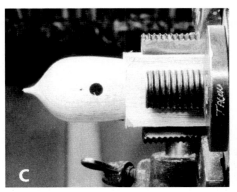

After the body is turned, hollowed and friction-fit on waste block, it's ready for final turning and sanding.

Using the parting tool, cut off the birdhouse body to the appropriate length.

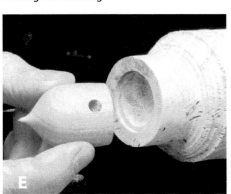

Prior to refining the rest of the birdhouse cap, check the fit of the cap to the body of the birdhouse ornament.

Once the fit to the cap is snug, refine cap shape with the spindle gouge. Entry and perch holes are already drilled.

Once the fit to the cap is snug, use the spindle gouge to refine the shape of the acorn cap.

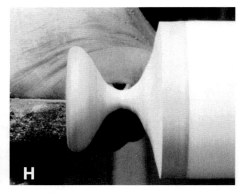

Prior to parting it from the lathe, refine the shape of the acorn cap with a 3/8" spindle gouge.

At this point, the cap has been parted from the lathe, reversed and friction-fit to the waste block, allowing final shaping and drilling of a screw eye hole for hanging.

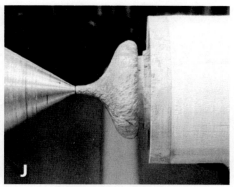

Complete the cap held in place with the tail center.

Use a small round skew to refine the ebony perch.

fit into the hole you drilled into the acorn body, and part off the perch. Cyanoacrylate glue holds the perch in place.

For finish, spray the acorn birdhouse with a satin or semi-gloss lacquer.

Now, try something smaller

Once you become accomplished at turning the bird houses, consider a variation or two. One variation that I have found to be a good seller is an acorn you can fashion into a necklace or earrings. Except for size, the process for turning these miniatures is exactly the same as for the larger acorn birdhouse. For the

body stock, I start out with 1/2" stock about 1-1/2" long and cap stock about 1" square by 3/4" long that can be glued to a waste block for turning. This is a great way to use up those small precious pieces of wood that you can't bear to throw away, and if you do manage to blow it up, you have wasted very little.

The holes for the birdhouse entry and the perch should be appropriate to the size of the finished piece. The birdhouse entry hole should be something less than 1/8" and the perch hole about 1/32". My only caution here would be to pay attention to proportion. It's very easy to turn a perch that's simply too large for the finished piece or to drill an entry

Turn a globe at one end of the perch to help insert this small piece.

hole that is either too large or too small or to make a cap that just doesn't look like it belongs.

Bob Rosand is a professional turner and educator living in Bloomsburg, PA. He has been a frequent contributor to the AW Journal.

Inside-Out Bottle Ornament

Michael Werner

Here are two ornaments based on inside-out turning techniques.

The wine-bottle ornament shown here is based on a full-size "2002 Vintage" wine bottle with turned grapes inside, which I demonstrated in 2005 at the Overland Park symposium. I first became intrigued with this technique after translating an inside-out turning article (sometimes called split turning) by a good friend of mine, Swiss master turner Sigi Angerer. After some practice,

I combined his technique with Michael Hosaluk's playful approach to turning.

Traditionally, all inside-out turnings are made from four square pieces of wood and one or more inside element. The goblet, olives, apples, pears, candles, and so on are just smaller versions of something you have perhaps already practiced turning.

AW 21:4, p54

Get started

For turning, I use a 1/2" spindle gouge, 3/8" detail gouge, 1" skew, 3/8" beading tool, and 1/8" parting tool.

For small turnings like these, I prefer to turn with a safety drive center at the headstock and a live center at the tailstock. The preference for the safety drive center over a 4-jaw chuck is for safety reasons and the ability to get my tool rest closer to the work.

For precise measuring, I suggest a machinist's caliper. An awl and automatic center punch come in handy to mark centers.

To prepare the material to square stock, access to a tablesaw, planer, or both is a must, and a bandsaw is helpful.

In traditional preparation to split the turning later, newspaper or brown craft paper (grocery bags) separates the four segments.

For these projects, I used poplar because it is lightweight and takes color quite well. If you plan on more intricate inside turnings, a harder-grained wood (maple or cherry) will be a better choice.

Use clamps, tape, or rubber bands to hold the segments while the glue dries. I've found that yellow woodworker's glue works well for this technique.

Sketches and drawings are critical in any turning process. I suggest you make many different concept sketches of your inside-out turning projects.

Observe all standard rules of safe turning and follow the manufacturer's guidelines for paint and color applications.

Wine Bottle Ornament

Finished size: 7 x 1-7/8" (180 x 48mm).

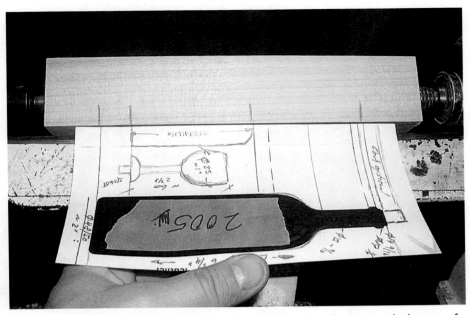

Transferring the dimensions onto the turning stock. Note the small spigot on the bottom of the goblet. The "research" wine bottle for this shape came from New Zealand—all the pattern dimensions were upside-down!

Begin on the inside

For the wine bottle ornament, I used a different approach. I made this piece from a solid 2" square. After turning what would become the inside, I cut the stock into four quarters on a bandsaw. This time-saving approach is useful for a simple project like an ornament, but you lose stock the width of the kerf in the process.

A fundamental guideline for all inside-out pieces: The smallest diameter of the inside shape should not be less than 60 percent of the finished outside diameter. Using the large wine bottle as an example, the maximum outside diameter (OD) is 1-7/8" (48mm), and the minimum inside diameter is 1-1/8" (28mm). If the inside diameter is less, the piece will fall apart when you turn the outside.

Transfer the template dimensions to the stock. With a skew and spindle gouge, turn the inside shape.

Check the contour shape of the opening from the flat side of the part—not the corner. To finish these simple, nearly square openings, I found a 3/8" beading tool (similar to a wide parting tool in profile) to be the most steady.

Remember that sanding this portion with square corners on each side can whack your knuckles. Always move the tool rest out of the way and use it to rest your hands on for better control while sanding. From scrap stock, turn a goblet about 2 × 1".

Apply inside color

With acrylic paint or aniline dye, color the inside of the bottle and wine glass. (Choose from many colors and brands of acrylic paints at hobby and crafts stores.) After the paints or stains dry thoroughly, cut the solid block into quarters using the bandsaw and bandsaw fence.

Install the wine goblet and glue the four sections together. Apply the glue carefully on the inside portion of the bottle, as glue squeeze-out will be difficult to remove. Allow the glue to dry completely under clamp pressure.

Turn the outside

Make sure your lamination is centered exactly between the drive and live centers. Using the outside template, mark the important dimensions. Instead of using your roughing gouge, try turning with a spindle gouge using a slicing motion. (Cut the turning stock at 45 degrees, mimicking a skew.) Or, rely on tools you're comfortable with at your lathe.

Clean cutting and the correct rpm are essential, as sanding on the lathe is not possible in the section with the opening. (It's not safe, and your crisp edges will be rounded over.) Off the lathe, sand with the grain to 220 smoothness.

Because aniline dye or stain will accent scratches, you may find it necessary to resand and apply stain a second time. If you apply color on the lathe with pens, slow down the lathe speed to about 100 rpm. Doing so will extend the life of the points.

For the final coat of finish, spray on a clear coat of satin finish.

For a hanger, use green floral wire (available at most crafts stores or nurseries) or similar thin wire. Adhere the wire with cyanoacrylate (CA) glue.

The Olive Jar Ornament

Finished size: 2-3/4 × 1-1/4" (70 x 32mm). This project stretches the red and green holiday theme, yet it's no less fun.

Begin on the inside

Cut four pieces of poplar to 3-1/2 × 5/8" × 5/8". To help center the work, sand a 1/16" chamfer on the interior corner of each block. Mark the pieces as shown in the drawing.

A 3/8" beading tool (also called a European beading tool) is ideal for scraping the inside portion of the wine bottle. Note the 60 percent diameter dimensions for this ornament taped to the tool rest as a reminder. This proportion follows the guidelines for inside-out turning.

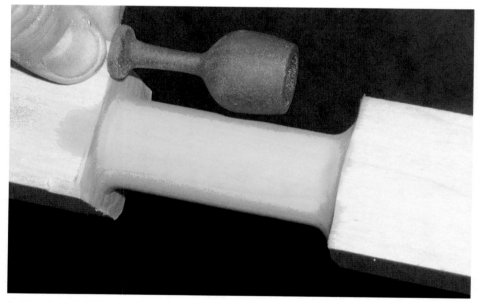

Aniline dye colors the inside of this ornament. Note how the corners are filed down 45 degrees to make room for the spigot of the goblet.

Glue the four pieces, using craft paper to separate each. Use yellow woodworker's glue and apply to the length of each piece. Clamp and allow glue to dry.

Turn the inside shape using the techniques described and the template for reference.

Apply color

Use acrylic paint to paint the olives and the inside of the jar. Mount the olives on the floral wire and arrange in one of the jar halves. Follow the procedures described in earlier steps to glue and clamp the jar halves.

Complete the outside

To turn close to the work, attach a waste block to an arbor screw chuck and turn a precise, shallow recess for the square glue-up. Cut the bottom end of the jar blank square, and adhere to the waste block with CA glue. With a spindle gouge, turn the outside of the jar to approximately 2-3/4 × 1-1/4".

Sand and finish the project with acrylic paint. If you wish, date the jar as shown.

Parting (and splitting) thoughts

Part of exploring is practice, practice, and practice. The technique of inside-out or split turning has many other possibilities in artistic and furniture applications.

As for the research for the shape of the wine bottles: Enjoy the glass of wine but remember to turn responsibly.

Michael Werner, a Swiss native, lives in Stanwood, Washington. He is a professional woodturner and teaches manufacturing technology (think shop) at a local high school.

Cut the solid block into quarters along the fence on the bandsaw.

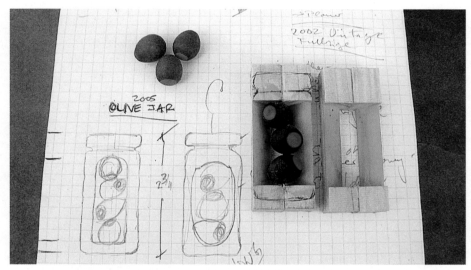

Before regluing the olive jar, apply color to the two halves and the olives. Note the full-size sketches and dimensions available for handy reference.

You'll find most of the finishing supplies for these ornaments at crafts stores, including colored markers, acrylic paints, and brushes designed for acrylic paints.

Wine Bottle Patterns

Patterns shown at 60%. For full scale, enlarge by 167%.

INSIDE END VIEW

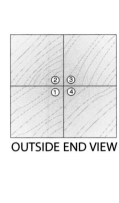

OUTSIDE END VIEW

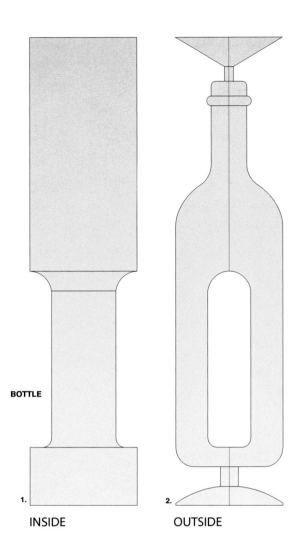

BOTTLE

1.

INSIDE

2.

OUTSIDE

Olive Jar Patterns

1.

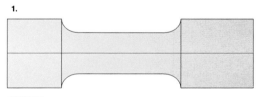

INSIDE

2.

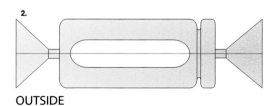

OUTSIDE

INSIDE END VIEW

OUTSIDE END VIEW

Patterns shown at 60%. For full scale, enlarge by 167%.

Ornaments from Tube Kits

Joshua Friend

This simple project is sure to please during the holidays: ornaments from a tube kit. There are many projects that make use of brass tubes for centering and driving the wood on the lathe, such as pens, whistles, letter openers, and perfume atomizers. If you have not yet ventured into the world of tube kits, this project is a good place to start. It's simple, quick, and fun!

There are several resources for purchasing ornament kits. I bought mine from Craft Supplies USA.

When you purchase an ornament kit, it comes with a brass tube, a decorative tip (in the shape of a droplet, icicle, or spiral), and an eye cap for hanging the ornament *(Photo 1)*. You will also need a pen mandrel, which is used for holding and driving the piece on the lathe, and two bushings, which make it easy to achieve a smooth transition from the wood to the metal parts *(Photo 2)*. When ordering, make sure to purchase the 7 mm (.335") bushings,

the appropriate size for this kit. You will also need a 7 mm drill bit.

Wood preparation

This project does not require much wood, so it is ideal for using up small scraps or pieces of exotic wood or burl. The brass tube provided in the kit determines the length of the blank: The wood should be cut about ¼" (6mm) longer than the brass tube. Place the brass tube on the wood and make a cut mark so that about ⅛" (3mm) overhangs each

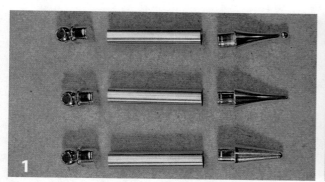

Ornament kits can be purchased in three styles, top to bottom: droplet, icicle, spiral.

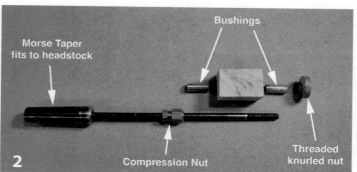

A typical pen mandrel can be used to turn many different tube-type kits. The bushings go on both sides of the wood and provide a target diameter for a smooth wood-to-kit transition when the kit is assembled.

AW 28:5, p21

end *(Photo 3)*. It is not essential to cut the wood square because the blank will be squared up later using a barrel trimmer. The width of the blank depends on your design.

Drill a hole all the way through the blank using a 7-mm drill bit. Center the hole, but precision is not absolutely necessary because the blank will become centered when it is turned *(Photo 4)*.

Prior to gluing the brass tube into the wood, gently rough up the surface of the tube using a fine abrasive, which will improve adhesion of metal to wood. I usually make multiples of these kits, so to make the process efficient, I insert a flap sander into my drill press and apply the tube to it, wearing gloves, of course *(Photo 5)*. Hand sanding with a small piece of 220-grit abrasive will also do the trick.

Glue the tube into the wood so that the tube is slightly recessed on both ends. Several types of glue can be used, but my favorite is two-part epoxy, which provides plenty of working time and a strong bond. Another type of adhesive that would give similar benefits is polyurethane glue. If you are in a hurry, use CA glue, but beware of its quick setting time: If you don't position the tube quickly, it could end up glued into the wrong place. If this happens, additional tubes can be purchased separately.

Apply glue directly to the brass tube and work the tube into the hole, twisting it in and out to spread the glue evenly *(Photo 6)*. You can purchase an insertion tool designed for helping push the tube inside the wood and into the proper position, but I find it sufficient to use the end of a pencil or other pointed object such as a scratch awl.

The tube is set inside the wood because, after the glue cures, the wood will be trimmed down flush and square with the tube. This must be done prior to turning the project on the lathe so that later, when the ornament's brass fittings are pressed into the tube, the wood will be square and you will have a good union from wood to metal (no gaps).

There are various methods of trimming the wood flush with the tube, but I like to use a barrel trimmer because it is simple, easy, and consistent. The pilot shaft of the barrel trimmer goes inside the brass tube and aligns the cutter head square to it. Make sure to cut down far enough so that the brass tube is freshly exposed. It is okay to trim a little bit off the end of the brass tube because that will ensure the wood and tube are flush and square with the length of the tube itself *(Photo 7)*. Do this on both ends of the workpiece.

Mounting and turning

Now you are ready to take the project to the lathe. Mount the Morse taper of the mandrel into the lathe's headstock. Refer to *Photo 2*, which shows the order in which the pieces must go onto the mandrel. Most mandrels come with a compression nut or locking collar so you can adjust the position of your workpiece on the mandrel. It should be positioned far enough to the end so you can tighten down the knurled nut with moderate pressure. Bring up the tailstock with the point of a live center or a 60° cone and apply light pressure to the end of the mandrel. Too much pressure from the tailstock will result in bending the mandrel and it will not turn true.

This is a good opportunity to work on a variety of spindle-turning skills. Although the project is small, I like to start with a roughing gouge to round the piece to a cylinder. Do this by holding the handle of the gouge down so that you are rubbing the bevel without cutting. Then, slowly and gently lift the handle until the

Cut the wood about 1/4" longer than the brass tube, allowing for 1/8" of wood beyond each end of the tube.

Drill a 7 mm hole through the wood. A wooden clamp will suffice to hold the piece, but specialized pen-drilling vises are available.

Lightly sand the brass tube before gluing it into the wood.

Spread the glue evenly on the brass tube and make sure the tube is below the wood's surface on both ends.

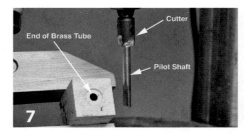

A barrel trimmer makes quick work of trimming the wood flush and square with the brass tube.

cutting edge is engaged. Point the cutting edge slightly in the direction of the cut and move the tool from center to end *(Photos 8, 9).*

After the piece is round, I use a spindle gouge to turn various details such as beads, coves, ridges, or tapers. In general, all details formed on the lathe fall into the broad categories of coves, beads, and fillets (flats). Seeing it this way, the outside of a bowl, for example, is part of a large bead, and a taper on a spindle is part of a gradual cove. It's an interesting way to think about forms and design.

These ornament kits allow you to creatively pursue shapes and designs *(Photos 10, 11).* You can even cut all the way down to the brass tube to achieve a contrast between wood and metal *(Photo 12).* But, there is one important consideration: the bushings are the same diameter as the brass fittings on the kit. So, whatever transition you use for the wood to the bushings is the transition the wood will make to the brass fittings in final assembly.

When you have achieved a design you are happy with, sand the piece *(Photo 13).* Fine details should be sanded with fine abrasive (320 or 400 grit) so that details remain crisp. If you rely on heavy sanding to remove torn wood grain or frayed edges, you will end up with muted details.

Finishing up
Apply your favorite finish, such as a friction polish or wax applied

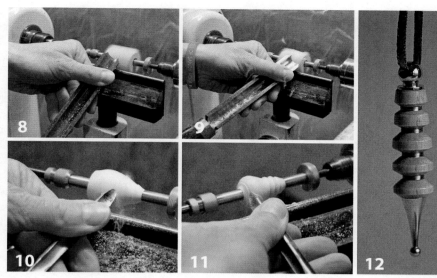

The fundamentals of spindle turning are: anchor the tool on the toolrest, rub the bevel, and then engage the cutting edge.

Ornaments provide an opportunity to practice the techniques of spindle turning.

Cutting deep enough to expose the brass tube provides a contrast between wood and metal.

on the lathe. I like to use a sprayed gloss lacquer. To spray the workpiece without having to touch it, I mount it on a dowel with a small amount of electrical tape on each end to hold it in place, and then I simply hold the dowel and spray *(Photo 14).* Suspend the ends of the dowel on a rack while the finish dries.

The final step is to assemble the kit parts. The decorative tip and end cap are designed for a press fit, which means no glue is needed. There are several means of applying pressure to achieve a press fit, such as a vise or a drill press—both fitted with scrap wood to protect the kit—a clamp, or a pen press designed specifically for this type of application. Press in either the decorative tip or end cap

first, but not both at the same time. Apply slow, gentle pressure until the brass of the fitting seats squarely with the wood *(Photo 15).*

Now you are ready to surprise friends and family with a lovely ornament. Alternatively, these kits can also be used to make decorative pulls for light-fixture chains.

Joshua Friend, a woodturner and writer, is a member of the Nutmeg Woodturners League, an AAW chapter that meets in Brookfield, Connecticut.

Gently sand with the toolrest out of the way.

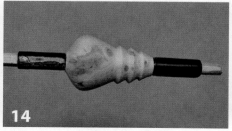

A dowel rod makes an easy setup for spray finishing small kit parts.

Scrap wood mounted in a vise will protect the brass fittings while slowly press-fitting pieces together.

Made in the USA
Monee, IL
16 October 2020